19301

The Power of Positive Preaching to the Lost

John R. Bisagno

The Power of Positive Preaching to the Lost

BROADMAN PRESS
Nashville, Tennessee

PREFACE

These sermons are not presented as polished literary gems. They are simple, direct, hard-hitting revival sermons as actually preached in the heat of revivals in some of America's outstanding evangelistic churches.

CONTENTS

1

The Unpardonable Sin

"Then was brought unto him one possessed with a devil, blind, and dumb: and he healed him, insomuch that the blind and dumb both spake and saw.

"And all the people were amazed, and said, Is not this the son of David?

"But when the Pharisees heard it, they said, This fellow doth not cast out devils but by Beelzebub the prince of the devils.

"And Jesus knew their thoughts, and said unto them, Every kingdom divided against itself is brought to desolation; and every city or house divided against itself shall not stand: And if Satan cast out Satan, he is divided against himself; how shall then his kingdom stand?

"And if I by Beelzebub cast out devils, by whom do your children cast them out? therefore they shall be your judges.

"But if I cast out devils by the Spirit of God, then the kingdom of God is come unto you.

"Or else how can one enter into a strong man's house, and spoil his goods, except he first bind the strong man? and then he will spoil his house.

"He that is not with me is against me; and he that gathereth not with me scattereth abroad.

"Wherefore I say unto you, All manner of sin and blasphemy shall be forgiven unto men: but the blasphemy against the Holy Ghost shall not be forgiven unto men.

"And whosoever speaketh a word against the Son of man, it shall be forgiven him, but whosoever speaketh against the Holy Ghost it shall not be forgiven him, neither in this world, neither in the world to come.

"Either make the tree good, and his fruit good; or else make the tree corrupt, and his fruit corrupt; for the tree is known by his fruit.

"Oh generation of vipers, how can ye being evil, speak good things? For out of the abundance of the heart the mouth speaketh" (Matt. 12:22-34).

It's bad enough to think that men would sin against a Holy God and necessitate the overwhelming forgiving grace of God. But to think that men would so sin as to never be forgiven, is almost beyond the realm of comprehension. And yet the Bible clearly says that one such unforgivable, unpardonable sin clearly exists.

If you knew that this night you would commit a sin that would finally and eternally seal your destiny in hell, would you do it? The answer, of course, is no! Yet, many of you listening to me are standing in the very shadows of the unpardonable sin. It is not an uncommon sin; it is not a sin relegated to the archives of antiquity. To the contrary, it is perhaps America's most prevalent sin. It is not adultery, murder, lying, stealing, or drunkenness. It is simply this: "Blasphemy against the Holy Ghost shall not be forgiven unto men."

It is nothing more and nothing less. To this there can be no question, no controversy. The question is, what is blasphemy against the Holy Spirit? And to this there is much controversy. To understand the answer to this tricky question, as to every controversial theological question, one must understand the context in which Jesus said that a man could sin so as to never be forgiven.

One day the disciples brought a man, who was blind and mute, to the Master. The man was demon possessed. This does not mean that blindness and muteness are always signs of demon possession, but in this particular case it was. Without prayer lines or healing cloths, Jesus healed the man. He healed him instantly, publicly, and completely. Immediately, all the people were amazed and said, "Is this not the son of David?" Among other things, when the Messiah, the Savior was to come, he was to be called the Son of God, the Son of man, the Son of Abraham, the Son of David and many other names. He was to validate his ministry by the performing of miracles. Verse 23, instead of saying all the people were amazed, literally says, and most all of the people were amazed and said, "See, here is the Messiah. We are convinced by these miracles; we believe his power; we acknowledge him." In other words, when most of the people witnessed the preaching, the ministry, the miracles in force, the power of Jesus Christ, they were convicted. They said, "We believe he is the Messiah, the Son of God, the Son of David."

Today, it is the same. Most people who continually go to a gospel preaching church and constantly witness the ministry and power of Jesus Christ carried out and attested to by the power of the Holy Spirit, are likewise converted. The problem is that most people never hear the gospel of Jesus Christ. They hear positive thinking, good living, history lessons, Ann Landers, weather reports, but few, far too few, ever hear the blood bought old-fashioned new birth, hell and heaven, crucified, resurrected, interceding, soon returning gospel of Jesus Christ. Then, as now, when most people were touched by the message and ministry of Jesus Christ, they accepted him and were saved. But verse 24 continues, when the Pharisees heard it, they said, "Oh, no, this fellow, this carpenter has no heavenly power. He is not the Son of God, the promised Messiah; this power is the devil's power." They, once and for all, crossed off Jesus Christ and the power in him as being of the devil.

Who were these Pharisees? Were they seeing the power of God and hearing his gospel for the first time? Most people are saved the first time they are touched by the power of heaven, but they had probably been following Jesus every day for three years and the more they heard, the harder they became. Now, remember this, the biggest lie Satan will ever get you to believe is that by waiting and by tasting more and more of the gospel, by coming closer and closer, you will become easier and your heart will become softer. It is a lie; you will not. You get harder. The most easily you could have ever been converted was the first time you heard the gospel. The more you wait, the harder you become. Every passing day brings an increasing resistance to the gospel. The same sun that melts the ice, also hardens the clay.

Delay is danger and death. Most people are converted early in their life. I repeat; for your soul's sake hear it well. When the devil tells you to put it off, it will be easier, he lies! It will become harder. Every day it will become harder. This is the time. Now is the hour; today is the day of salvation. The Pharisees had countless opportunities to accept Christ, but the more the Holy Spirit called them, and drew them through the ministry of Jesus Christ, the harder they became.

The first time you brand a cow it will writhe in agony. But if you keep hitting that same spot with a branding iron, it will eventually become so hardened, so calloused, that it will make no response at all. This is what the Pharisees did and they finally blasphemed, insulted, rejected, and repelled the ministry of the Holy Spirit through Jesus Christ one last time. They got the last call from God and God gave them up. They crossed the deadline and crossed Jesus off and his whole ministry and power as of being of the devil and God said, "Let them alone."

There are only two powers in this world, the power of God and the power of Satan. If you honor the power of God, the drawing power of the Holy Spirit pulling you to Jesus Christ by accepting him, by yielding to him, you will be saved. But if you insult, repulse, and reject him, you acknowledge only the power of Satan as the god and the reigning power over your life and commit the unpardonable sin.

Verse 25 says that Jesus knew their thoughts. This is the key to the unpardonable sin. Jesus knew what they were thinking. The unpardonable sin is not in the mouth, it is in the heart. It is not something man says, it is something man does. The mouth is the fruit, but the heart is the root. The unpardonable sin is crucifying the Holy Ghost. It is going to church, hearing the gospel being preached and witnessed to and in one hundred other ways being called by the Holy Spirit to repentance and faith in Jesus Christ and having the audacity, after hearing, to say no to him. "No, I am not ready to come; don't crowd me; I'll come when I am ready."

Unfortunately, most people think that the unpardonable sin must be spoken, that it must be a verbal insult of the Holy Spirit. Their reason is that verse 32 says, "And whosoever speaketh against the Holy Spirit, it shall not be forgiven him." But look again at that statement in context. In verse 31 Jesus says simply, clearly, and finally that blasphemy against the Holy Ghost shall not be forgiven unto men. PERIOD! If this were the only verse in the Bible, it should be clear, once and for all, that speaking against the Holy Spirit is not the unpardonable sin, but that it is only a symptom of the fact that the unpardonable sin has already been committed in their heart. Having said, once and for all, in verse 31, that blasphemy against the Holy Spirit is the unpardonable sin, Jesus adds something else in verse 32. He now says, carrying out the thought, "And now I am going to tell you something else in addition to that; not only is blasphemy against the Holy Spirit unforgivable, if you speak against the Holy Spirit, *that is unpardonable, too.*" Why? He explains it in verses 33 and 34. The man who speaks against him has already blasphemed against him in his heart. What men say with their mouth is only the symptom of what they have already said in their heart. To be sure, one who speaks against the Holy Spirit has committed the unpardonable sin, but he is only evidencing the fact that he has already blasphemed him in his heart, not in the mouth. The heart is the root, the mouth is the fruit. He says in verse 33 that with the fruit of their mouth they could not bring forth any good praises to him. They could say nothing good about him because their sterile, impotent, empty-hearted hearts could produce nothing good and adds in verse 34, "O generation of vipers." Literally he was saying, "Oh, you barrel of rattlesnakes, you are so empty-hearted and empty-headed, so abjectly devoid of everything good that you could not say anything good if you wanted to. For out of the abundance of the heart, the mouth speaketh. It was absolutely impossible from that day to eternity for the Pharisees ever again to say anything good about Jesus. They could not honor him with their lips, they could not confess him with their words. They could not accept him with their mouth because their hearts had crossed the deadline. They had waited too long. They had built up an indestructible, unbreakable resolve against God in their hearts. They were eternally, irrevocably, locked in the sin of Christ rejection, forever locked in the condition of their hardened heart, sealed in their own damnation, and forever consigned to hell.

The unpardonable sin is blasphemy against the Holy Ghost. Two questions arise: What is blasphemy? Who is the Holy Ghost?

1. To blaspheme means to insult something sacred and need not necessarily be spoken. Suppose I were to come inside your church next Sunday morning and roll up the rugs and have a dance and put on a big drunken blast in the sanctuary. I would be insulting your auditorium which has been sanctified to the glory of God. I would be blaspheming the sanctuary, but blasphemy against the sanctuary is not the unpardonable sin. Were I to take the sacred vessels of the Lord's Supper table and desecrate and mock them by getting drunk out of them, I would be insulting, blaspheming, the sacred vessels. But blasphemy against the Lord's Supper table is not the unpardonable sin. If I were to come into your educational building and write obscene words all over the walls, I would be blaspheming that building, but blasphemy against the educational building is not the unpardonable sin. In every sense, I

would be blaspheming without saying a word. Blasphemy is not necessarily what one says; it is what one does. Blasphemy means insulting something that is sacred and holy.

2. To understand why this final rejection of his ministry is unforgivable, we must answer the question, "Who is the Holy Ghost and what is his ministry?" This mysterious, delicate third member of the Godhead has many ministries. To the Christian he does the actual work of regeneration in the life of the believer. He seals and keeps him for eternity. To the Christian he speaks, comforts, guides, teaches, convicts, helps, and interprets, and performs innumerable of his ministries. With the unsaved person, however, he has only one job, just one ministry. The purpose of the Holy Spirit, that only ministry for which he exists with the lost man, woman, boy or girl, is to draw them to Jesus Christ. He exists for no other purpose with you. The unpardonable sin is simply this: If in your pride, your self-sufficiency, your arrogance, and rebellion against God, you habitually refuse to allow him to do the one thing he is in the world to do, to draw you to Jesus Christ, eventually he will simply withdraw and leave you alone in your sins and you will have crossed the deadline.

Contrary to what you may believe, you cannot be saved any time you are good and ready. Over and over the Bible emphasis is on salvation *today!* Today, if you will hear his voice, harden not your heart, as in the day of provocation. There is no tomorrow on God's calendar, and you cannot be saved just anytime. You can insult the Holy Spirit one last time; you can say no to him so long that he will eventually say no to you. He will eventually reject you. You can crucify the

Holy Ghost. In Genesis, God said, "My Spirit will not always strive with man." And Jesus added, "Except the Father that sent me draw him, no man can come unto me."

Three times in the first chapter of Romans the Bible says, "God gave them up." God gave them up! God gave them up! Do you think you will be saved when you are ready? "Don't push me, I'll come when I am ready," says the lost man. If I have heard it once, I have heard it a thousand times. But what are you going to do if you get ready and he is not ready? There are two points in a man's life between which he may be saved. He cannot come before, he cannot come after. No man knows where either of them is, that is why the invitation is always today!

The first point comes when you reach the age of accountability. Some come to an awareness of their sins and a conviction of their need of Christ at age six, at seven or eight, or even ten, fifteen, or twenty. No one can say when different individuals reach the age of accountability. The same uncertainty surrounds the unpardonable sin. Can you be sure you will have three chances or four or five or ten or twenty? Perhaps you can hear the gospel for six months before the Holy Spirit quits striving with you, perhaps it will be a year, or five, or twenty, or fifty. No one can say. There is only one time that it is safe for you to be saved, and that is now; today; this minute; before you finish reading this page. Even the printed words of this chapter may be the last extended call of the Holy Spirit to your soul. At this moment you may be one step away from committing the unpardonable sin, one page short of crossing the deadline. Today, today, today, receive him today. The unpardonable sin is a sin of delay.

The searching, forgiving Savior is seeking us! Wonder of wonders, amazing grace, how amazing. But if in your pride, you persistently harden your heart, and you the creature have the audacity to say no to the Creator, what he does is to simply abide by your decision and leave you eternally in a condition without him.

The Hebrew writer has stated, "He that despised Moses' law died without mercy under two or three witnesses. Of how much more punishment suppose ye, shall ye be thought worthy who have trampled under foot the blood of the covenant and have done despite to the Spirit of Grace?" Man, you would be far better off to bite your tongue in half and spit it out of your head than to say no to God. Does it seem a light thing to you in his sight? You are stomping over the cross and defying, despising the Holy Spirit. I have talked to hundreds of men about Christ and seen them, after hours of pleading still say no. And though I have never done it, I have felt like saying to them, "Man, if you have made up your mind to go to hell, go ahead; I am through with you." If I can feel that way, when I am not even the one who is being rejected, I can see why the Father would say to the Holy Spirit, "Leave him alone, don't call him anymore; he has insulted me for the last time. He has crossed the deadline."

The unpardonable sin is a sin against light; it is a sin against knowledge, a sin against opportunity. I believe the Bible teaches degrees of punishment in hell. You would be far better off to die and go to hell from the jungles of Africa, where you have had little light, little possibility of salvation than to go to hell from America, where there is a church on every street corner. Some shall be beaten with few stripes and some with many. To whom much is given, much shall be required.

What about the people in Africa, who have not heard the gospel? Do they have a chance? I do not know! But my question is, "What about you that have heard it ten thousand times? What excuse will you give? Do you really think that when you stand before God and say, "Lord, there were hypocrites in the church," or "Lord, I was a good man," or "Lord, I was going to be saved," that the Lord will say, "Is that right? Well, what do you know. Then come on in since there were hypocrites in the church, I'll let you in anyway." Of course not. Oh, sinner, I beg of you, be saved today.

The unpardonable sin is a sin of the will. Regardless of what you say, regardless of what excuse you tell me, it is not the feeling you are waiting for, it is not anything except one thing: You are lost because you *will* to be lost! You are not saved because you *will* not be saved. God has made man above the angels, above animals and matter; he has made you with a will. You can choose to respond to the Spirit's calling or you may choose against him.

The unpardonable sin is a sin of the will. Jesus wept over Jerusalem in the night of their rejection. Hear him as he cries, "Oh, Jerusalem, Jerusalem, thou that stonest the prophets and killest them that are sent unto thee. How oft would I have gathered you unto myself as a hen gathers her brood under her wing, but ye would not." He did not say, you could not or ye did not or you may not, but "Ye would not." You can be saved if you want to be saved. There is no reason in the world for you to go on lost in darkness, destined for hell. You can be saved if you will to be saved. Stop delaying, quit making excuses; come now. You can be saved if you will!

The unpardonable sin is a sin against *compassion.* When you cross the deadline, when the burden of the Holy Spirit is withdrawn from your life, it will be withdrawn from others who have cared about you.

Many years ago in a small northeastern city, we had spent over eight hours one week trying to win a man to Christ. He kept saying, "No, preacher, not now, I am not ready." The pastor had tried to win him to Christ for 14 years, his wife for 20 years. Always it was the same, "Not today, I will do it tomorrow." After an all-night prayer meeting one Saturday I met his wife in the hall during Sunday School and she looked very refreshed and called to me. "Thank God," I said, "you've got the victory, your husband is going to be saved this morning?" "No," she said, "and preacher, it's a strange thing, I just don't care any more. God has removed the burden." Quickly I raced to the pastor's office and said, "Pastor, come quickly, Frank has committed the unpardonable sin. God has removed the burden from his wife. We must go to him one more time." "I can't go," he replied. "This morning as I was praying, the burden lifted. I am sorry to say it, but I simply don't care anymore." With that he turned and walked away. When you cross the deadline, when the Holy Spirit withdraws from your life and leaves you eternally and irrevocably locked in your decision of rejection, he will remove the burden from the hearts of others who have loved and prayed for you. But remember this: Though you will first have every opportunity, you will never know when the last opportunity may come! The Bible tells us that God hardened Pharaoh's heart. Many people have tried to preach around this, to explain it away. The truth of the matter is that God did harden Pharaoh's heart, but he gave him ten chances to repent first!

The unpardonable sin is a sin against *faith*. The biggest lie the devil will ever tell you is that you will know when your time comes to be saved, that you will feel it. Men are not saved by feeling, they are saved by faith. God did not say that we have to have so much money to be saved, for some are rich and some are poor. He did not say that we have to have so much education, for some are educated and some are illiterate. But there is one thing that is common to all men. The ability to believe. You say you do not have faith, but every day you prove that you do. You ate something that someone else grew, cooked, prepared, and packaged. There may be poison in it, but still you ate it, in faith. You go to a doctor you have never seen before. He gives you a prescription you cannot read, you take it to a druggist whose name you cannot pronounce, he prepares a prescription you know nothing about, and yet you take it; all in faith. Yes, we exercise faith every day. The capacity to believe in Jesus Christ, to ask him to come into your heart by faith is the most prominent part of your personality. You can do it if you will, but you will never get that feeling you are waiting on. Why would God give you a feeling? What kind of a feeling would it be? How will you know it when it comes? You cannot trust your feelings, you cannot trust your emotions for they change. Will it be a feeling of elation? But some people do not get happy easily. Will it be a feeling of sorrow; will you cry? But that would not be fair for me for I do not weep easily, so God is not fair. Feelings change, they vary from person to person. Some do not show any feeling, so God would not be fair. Some people weep at funerals, some smile from inner peace. Hear me, for your soul's sake, hear me. Different people react to the same situation with different emotion, therefore, feelings cannot be trusted, emotions cannot be relied upon.

The unpardonable sin is a sin against *patience*. Throughout the history of the world, God has gone to great extent to call man to repentance, to get the good news through to him that he loves him and would pardon him. First, he spoke to man himself. But man blasphemed the Father, and rejected him. But God is long-suffering. "Perhaps they did not understand," he thought. "I will send men to give them the message in their own language." But they blasphemed the prophets, they did not hear him. Next, God sent the written Word that men could touch it, look at it, examine it, feel it, and see it, but the Bible says they blasphemed the Scriptures. They rejected even the written message.

Listen to the pathos, the agony from the great heart of God. "I will send my Son; surely they will reverence my Son." Now, the world has seen him in the flesh. God's love, God's forgiveness, his patience, his compassion wrapped in swaddling clothes, lying in a manger. Do they now believe? Do they now repent? Listen, "Release unto us Barabbas. Away with him. Let him be crucified."

The Bible says they blasphemed the Son, they rejected him, they insulted him. But oh, amazing grace, how sweet the sound. God has one last offer! Now, he sends the Holy Spirit; and on the day the Spirit of God burst upon the world scene in redeeming, drawing, convicting, saving grace God began his last appeal to man.

If you are waiting for perfection, it will not come.

If you are waiting for emotion, wait no more. If you are waiting for a new way of salvation, a new message, a new method, it is never coming. The Holy Spirit is God's last call.

To convict does not mean "to get an emotional feeling." It means to make aware of. Do you know you are lost? Yes! Do you know Christ died for you? Yes! Do you know you need to be saved? Yes! Do you intend someday to be saved? Yes! You are under conviction, only the Holy Spirit of God can make you aware of your need. Feelings and emotions will not come. Faith in answer to awareness is God's plan for your salvation. There is no other way.

The unpardonable sin is not the final blasphemous, insulting, rejection against the HOLY SPIRIT because he is the greatest. The unpardonable sin is against the HOLY SPIRIT because he is the latest. He is the last. There is no one else; there is nothing else; there will never be another plan, another way of your salvation.

2

Where Is Your Faith?

"And he answered and said unto them, My mother and my brethren are these which hear the word of God, and do it.

"Now it came to pass on a certain day, that he went into a ship with his disciples: and he said unto them, Let us go over unto the other side of the lake. And they launched forth.

"But as they sailed he fell asleep: and there came down a storm of wind on the lake; and they were filled with water, and were in jeopardy.

"And they came to him, and awoke him, saying, Master, master, we perish. Then he arose, and rebuked the wind and the raging of the water: and they ceased, and there was a calm.

"And he said unto them, Where is your faith? And they being afraid wondered, saying one to another, What manner of man is this! for he commandeth even the winds and water, and they obey him" (Luke 8:21-25).

The story is one of the most interesting in the Word of God. It tells of the disciples going across the sea with Jesus, and Jesus Christ calmly in the midst of the storm sleeping in the rear of the boat. His disciples, however, were afraid, they were troubled, because a storm had come upon the lake. Jesus stilled the storm when they were at the very point of death and they rejoice in his wonderful providence and protection. But at the end of the encounter Jesus seems to be very disappointed in them and asks the question, "Where is your faith?"

I want you to notice that he did not question whether they had faith or not. He knew they had faith. They had seen him raise the dead; they had seen him walk on water; they had seen him feed the five thousand. They had faith; they had plenty of faith. Everyone has faith. He was asking them where it was. There must be a recipient to the word "is." He knew they had faith. He asked, "Where is it?" "What have you done with it?" "What have you placed it in?"

And that's the question that I want to ask you. You're counting on something. You're depending on something. You're trusting in something to save you. You just can't be sailing through the sea of life without hope. Your trust is in something; yourself, your friends, your money, your future, tomorrow, your health, but these things aren't going to stand the test of life. Let's examine the question of Jesus. Where is your faith? And try to answer for ourselves.

First, we see here faith misplaced.

Where was their faith? Obviously, it was everywhere but where it was supposed to be. It seems to me that they must have had faith in themselves. They were old seamen. They were experienced sailors. What cared they for this land lover, this carpenter from Nazareth? He knew nothing of the water. They had not yet fully grasped that he was the God that had made the water. It was all right to keep Jesus in the back of the ship. It's all right to keep him in the back of your life. You're a pretty good fellow; you'll get along by yourself. You'll make it somehow. They had faith in themselves.

They were experienced seamen, and needed not this Christ.

Then it is obvious to me that they had faith in the water. Those peaceful quiet waters were the main thing in which they were trusting. And as long as on the solicitude of life one sails along smoothly on the quiet waters, he has nothing to worry about. But what are you going to do when the winds come, and the storms come, because life isn't like that? Life isn't a fantasy. Life doesn't go on endlessly. There are problems, and your faith is going to be tested. Ella Wheeler Wilcox was right when she said, "It's easy enough to be happy when the world goes by with a song, but the man who is worthwhile is the man who can smile when everything goes dead wrong." They had faith in themselves and they had faith in that water. They had faith in the quiet waters of life. Little did they know that before long, they would need Jesus, for things were not going to remain in that condition.

Then they surely had faith in the ship. They had built it; they had made it themselves. But would it stand the test of time? The frail bark of their own abilities, the fragile workings of their own hands, the pitch, the wood, the nails, would they hold together when trials and troubles came? They had faith in that ship. How foolish. How like many other people whose only faith is in the frail ship of life, in the ship of baptism, or the ship of church membership, or the ship of goodness, or the ship of emotion. They were trusting in that frail bark. And it was sure to fail them.

Secondly, we see, as is always the case, their faith tested. I want you to notice that the very thing that they trusted in the most was the first thing that turned upon them. The main thing that they were trusting in was the beautiful water. But that water came into the boat. That water was no longer their friend. It had become their enemy. They were not afraid of the land, they were not afraid of the sky. They were afraid of the water. The water that was once their friend was now their awesome enemy.

"Master, we perish." How did they think they were going to perish? They were afraid that they were going to drown. The water, their friend, was now their enemy. That very thing that you trust in, that very thing that you think is your strongest spot, may become your most vulnerable position. Most great men have had to be broken at their strongest point.

They say that every man knows his strength, and every man knows his weakness. And we say that the devil always hits us at our weaker spot. But many times the devil will hit you at your strength in your self-sufficiency. You're counting on your church membership, or you are counting on your ability to make money. But it may be the strongest man who will become the worst cripple. It may be the very strongest moral man who will become the most immoral man. It may be at the very point of your strength, that the very thing that you depend on the most will be the first thing to let you down.

The Bible says in that day many will be judged and their goodness tried, so as by fire. If any man's works be burned, he will suffer loss. If you are building on wood, hay, or stubble, they shall be dissolved. But unless you are building on the Rock of Ages, then those things that you are trusting in, the very strength of your life, will be the first thing to fail you. Peter had to lose his self-sufficiency, and Paul had to sacrifice his intellectualism to Christ's gospel.

Then their faith was tested by the storms, by the tremendous storm of wind that came down upon the lake. This speaks symbolically not only of the every-day difficulties of life, not only of the crumbling structure of our own goodness; but of those temptations, of those storms of passion that come into life un-announced. Death comes; sickness comes; injuries come; temptations come; divorce and financial reverses come. If you have tried to live without God, then you will find that when the storms of wind come into your life that you will have your faith like the disciples, mis-placed in the wrong thing.

Then their faith was tested by God himself. The Bible says in the book of Amos, "Prepare to meet thy God." God came face to face with these men. Oh, they were content to let Jesus sleep in one corner of the boat of their lives. They were content to eat their loaves and fishes. They were content to let him doze in one corner of the ship. But as soon as the storm came, they knew that God was in that storm and only God could help them. They were tested by God himself.

And then they were tested by the ultimate test, the test that every man faces, the test of death. Life is wonderful. Life is a beautiful experience. But at the end of it, there is death. And no matter who you are, or no matter how good you are, or what you have done in life, your goodness, your philosophy of life, is ultimately going to be tested by death itself. One day you are going to look in the face of death. And all of your goodness and all of your sins and all of your ex-cuses and all of your life will come up before you. It will be too late to be thinking about getting religion. Death, the ultimate test that comes to test every man's philosophy of life, is coming to you. They were afraid.

They were going to perish. They were going to die. Their faith, misplaced, was now tested by the ultimate test, the test of death.

Third and last, we see their faith replaced. They got smart. They woke up. They got some sense. They had time to make some changes. And thank God they did.

Their faith is now replaced. Notice when they replaced their faith that they came at the right time. They came while there was time. They didn't wait until they were in the water. They didn't wait until they had nearly drowned. They came when the storm was coming. They came at the right time.

Many years ago down in Arkansas I saw a sign on a beer joint that said "Free beer tomorrow." That's the way life is. It's always tomorrow. We'll do better tomorrow, we'll diet tomorrow. We'll exercise tomorrow; we'll be saved tomorrow; we'll start to church tomorrow; we'll start saving money tomorrow; we'll get a better job tomorrow; we'll start reading the Bible tomorrow. But the Bible never promises a tomorrow. It is always today. "Today if you hear his voice, harden not your hearts." Now is the hour. This is the accepted time. Thank God they came at the right time.

Then they came to the right person. They came to Jesus himself. They didn't come to a philosophy of life. They came to the Man, Jesus. If your faith is in the social teaching of Jesus, or in the church of Jesus, or in the philosophies of Jesus, then friend you are lost. You are wrong! You'll split hell wide open! Salvation is not in a preacher; it's not in a priest; it's not in a rabbi; it's not in a set of rules; it's not in the teachings of a book; it's not in a philosophical concept. Salvation is in a Man—the Man, Christ Jesus. The Bible says there is no other name under heaven given among men whereby we must be saved. They came to the right person. They came to Jesus Christ himself.

Then they came in the right way. They didn't come with a lot of big words. They didn't come with a lot of theology. They just said, "HELP! Save us, we perish!"

And notice, thank God, they got what they came after. What did they want? They wanted to be dry. Yes. They didn't want to have to swim to shore. That's right. They wanted a lot of things. But the main thing that they wanted was their skins saved. They wanted to live, and not die. They said, "Master, save us, we perish." And he did save them and they didn't drown. They got what they came after.

But, oh wonder of wonder, isn't it just like Jesus, they got more than they wanted. For the Bible says in the other accounts in the other Gospels, that immediately the ship was at the other side of the shore where it was going. Not only did he save them physically, but immediately there was a great calm, the waters subsided, the winds stopped blowing, and they were on the other side of the lake.

When Jesus saves a soul, he does a good job. When he comes into a life, he does it all. When he changes a heart, he completes the job. And he'll do the same thing for you today. Where is your faith?

If you are trusting in yourself, if you are trusting in the frail ship of life that you are building out of your own goodness, if you are trusting in the calm waters of life with no trouble yet, I warn you, troubles are going to come! Your faith will be tested: by God, by death, by difficulty. Replace your faith. Put it in Jesus. Come today, just as you are, and he will save you now.

3

The Great White Throne Judgment

"And I saw a great white throne, and him that sat on it, from whose face the earth and the heaven fled away; and there was found no place for them.

"And I saw the dead, small and great, stand before God; and the books were opened: and another book was opened, which is the book of life: and the dead were judged out of those things which were written in the books, according to their works.

"And the sea gave up the dead which were in it; and death and hell delivered up the dead which were in them: and they were judged every man according to their works.

"And death and hell were cast into the lake of fire. This is the second death.

"And whosoever was not found written in the book of life was cast into the lake of fire" (Rev. 20:11-15).

It goes without being said that God is a God of judgment. He judged the antediluvian age. He judged Adam when he sinned. The Bible tells us that God judged the angels. God judged Lucifer and banished him from heaven because of his war and rebellion against God. He judged the Roman Empire, he judged Hitler. The Bible tells us that God, the God of judgment, is coming again, taking vengeance and judgment on them that know not the Lord.

The Bible speaks of several distinct judgments. In

the future there will be the judgment of the Jews, the judgment of the nations, the judgment of the saved, and the judgment of the dead, to mention but a few.

In the Great White Throne judgment we are speaking specifically about the judgment of the unsaved.

First of all, who is going to be the judge? The Bible tells us that the Father judges no man but hath committed all judgment to the Son. The judge is going to be Jesus Christ himself. Think of it. That same Jesus of whom we sing "Jesus loves me, this I know, for the Bible tells me so"; and "Gentle Jesus, Holy Child, gentle Jesus, meek and mild." Yes, this very same Jesus who now offers himself to you as a Savior will one day be your judge.

Many years ago in San Francisco a young boy was riding down a hill on a homemade cart. Just as he was about to be struck by an automobile, a man threw himself in front of the car, saving the boy's life, and was himself injured. The young man grew up into a life of crime, and years later went before a judge for sentencing. The judge walked into the courtroom and the boy noticed that it was the same man that had saved his life. "How lucky I am," he thought. "This man saved my life once, and now he will save it again." But the man pronounced a sentence of death, and said, "Son, there was a time when I was your savior, but today I must be your judge."

When Jesus Christ came to this earth, he stood before Pilate. But when he comes again, Pilate is going to stand before him. I know it does a man a lot of good in his heart, it satisfies his pride and ego to sit in a congregation as judge and jury, and judge Jesus Christ as not worthy of your life, not worthy to be your Savior. But I warn you that the Bible says one day the tables are going to be turned. You are going to stand before Jesus, and what he does with you will be determined by what you have done with him. But in this service, you can settle it all. For he says, "Whosoever therefore shall confess me before men, him will I confess also before my Father which is in heaven. But whosoever shall deny me before men, him will I also deny before my Father which is in heaven" (Matt. 10:32-33).

The Bible says that in that day every knee shall bow and every tongue shall confess that Christ is Lord to the glory of the Father. You say, "Preacher, if I'm going to bow the knee anyway, then I'm going to be saved. Surely I'm going to have another opportunity." No, that's not what it means. God made you to honor and glorify Jesus Christ. And that's exactly what you are going to do. Now you may be forced to honor him as judge, or you may willingly bow your knee now before him as Savior. One way or another, however, you will give honor to Jesus Christ.

The Bible tells us that the Son of Man hath power on earth to forgive sins. That power operates here and now, in this life. If you now are willing to bow your knee before Christ and confess Christ as your Savior, that confession will be a confession unto salvation. But if you wait until judgment, when you confess him as judge, it will not be a confession of salvation. It will not save you; it will be too late. The only way you can be saved is now, today, tonight. I urge you to open your heart and acknowledge this Jesus Christ that you are rejecting, this Jesus that you refuse so glibly, whom you so casually look over as though he were just another man. But I warn you that you ARE going to bow your knee. One day the judge of all the earth shall come in vengeance and judgment, and this same Jesus is going to be the judge.

Secondly, who are going to be the judged? The Bible tells us in our text, "I saw the dead, small and great, stand before God." That word "dead" means the unsaved, the living dead, the dead, dead; those who are alive at the coming of Christ and those who are not, but are spiritually dead. The Bible says the wages of sin is death. Because you are a sinner, you are dead spiritually, separated from a loving and living God. And the dead, the unsaved, all of the lost, will stand before God. Now the Bible says "small and great." You say "Preacher, I can expect to see the bums, the no-goods, the immoral, the scoundrels, the rejects of the earth." But the Bible says the great as well, the kings, the priests, the potentates, the great, the high and the mighty, the rich, the movie stars, the elite, the high society crowd. All of the small and the great of this world who are spiritually dead will stand before God. Think of it. They will STAND before him.

In that day there will be no place to hide. Today men can come to a church and take refuge in the presence of others. They take refuge in the failures of others. I see people come to a service like this one, and they look at each other and laugh, they giggle, and punch each other in the ribs and hide and take great security in the fact that others do not go. But the Bible says on that day you are going to stand before God, Johnny on the spot. You will be alone!

The books will be opened; the books of opportunity of chances that you had to be saved. But it will be too late. You are going to be standing there before God by yourself, the dead, the unsaved, the small, the great, the good, the bad, the indifferent. "Whosoever's name that was not found written in the book of life, was cast into the lake of fire." The saved will not appear at this judgment. The born-again child of God will have already judged himself as guilty and as in need of a Savior. He has come to Christ and asked for mercy and received Jesus Christ as his Lord and Savior, his lawyer, and his defender. He will stand before a different judgment. At that judgment, the judgment seat of Christ, there will be no question about salvation, there will only be a question of faithfulness. Rewards will be given. Not for how many we won, not for how much good we do, but for how much good we did in relationship to how much we COULD have done. Whether we were good and faithful will not determine whether we go to hell or heaven, but it will determine the degree of our rewards in heaven. For our salvation will have already been determined.

The Bible says he that has received Christ has passed from death unto life. But the man that has not received Christ is condemned already. Whether you go to hell or heaven is determined now and here in this life. Not by your goodness, but by what you do with Jesus Christ. If you have rejected him you will have to stand before the GREAT WHITE THRONE JUDGMENT. If you have accepted him, you will stand before the judgment seat of Christ.

Third. Consider the judgment itself. As at any trial there are going to be witnesses. Many will come and witness against you. Now the Bible says that the books will be opened. This does not mean the book of your good works, for there will be no question of that. These will be the books that record the opportunities of your salvation. There will be one main book in which the blood of Christ will have written indelibly the name of all who have been born again by faith in Christ in this life. But there will be an awful blank, as an ugly socket from which a tooth has been extracted. There will be the empty place where your name might have been. I believe God will show you the blood of Christ and the pen of his love dipped in the blood ready to have written your name in the Lamb's book of life, but you would not come to Jesus Christ.

Then the books of opportunity will be opened. The witnesses will come. There will be unfolded across the silver screen of heaven the opportunities that you had to be saved.

The preachers may be called. "Lord, I did my best, I preached to him; I urged him to be saved." The Holy Spirit will come and witness against you. "Father, I tugged at his heart, night after night, I told him that he ought to be saved." There will be that witness, that faithful wife that prayed for you, that Sunday School teacher that loved you and tried to get you to come to Christ. But you would not come to Jesus.

There will be the Lord Jesus himself who will open his hands and show you his riven side and the scars on the palms of his hands and the pierced feet. And say, "Look, sinner, here are the hands, here is the opportunity, I wanted to save you. But you would not, you would not."

Then you will come and say, "But, Lord, I never had an opportunity." Jesus will say, "Just a minute." And he will say, "Start the projector across the silver screen of heaven," and there will come the evidence, the opportunities you had to be saved.

Some will come and say, "But Lord, no one ever told me." And Jesus will say, "Just a minute." And from the books will be the evidence of opportunities of time after time when someone came to you and asked you to be saved. And you would not. And then some will say, "But Jesus, I was a good man." Jesus will say, "Wait a minute, sinner, I did not say you had to be saved by being good. Remember that night I told you that you must be born again? And all of your righteousness was as filthy rags?" Some will say, "But Lord, I gave to the Red Cross. I gave to the church. I was this, I was that." "Whosoever's name was not found written in the book of life was cast into the lake of fire." "But Jesus, I intended to do it tomorrow." "Whosoever's name was not found written in the book of life was cast into the lake of fire." Some will come and say, "But Jesus, I never got the feeling." He will say, "I never told you to get a feeling, I told you to be saved by faith." "Whosoever's name was not found written in the book of life was cast into the lake of fire." "And oh, the weeping and the wailing, and the gnashing of teeth, as the lost are told of their fate."

The verdict? Guilty, guilty, guilty, over and over again! It will cry in your mind. Every diamond-studded nail from every clanking door of the penitentiary of the damned, as you are cast into the lake of fire, will say guilty, guilty, guilty! Every angel will bow his head and turn the other way, as you are bound hand and foot and are cast into hell. They, too, will cry guilty, guilty, guilty! Again the Bible says you are not going to be condemned, you are condemned already, now. Dead in transgressions and sin. Oh, what an awful day it will be.

4

The Conversion of a Thief

"And there were also two other, malefactors, led with him to be put to death.

"And when they were come to the place, which is called Calvary, there they crucified him, and the malefactors, one on the right hand, and the other on the left.

"And one of the malefactors which were hanged railed on him, saying, If thou be Christ, save thyself and us.

"But the other answering rebuked him, saying, Dost not thou fear God, seeing thou art in the same condemnation? And we indeed, justly; for we receive the due reward of our deeds: but this man hath done nothing amiss. And he said unto Jesus, Lord, remember me when thou comest into thy kingdom.

"And Jesus said, Verily I say unto thee, Today shalt thou be with me in paradise" (Luke 23:32-43).

Of course you will remember that the day that Jesus Christ was crucified there was not one, but three crosses on the hill called Calvary. There on each one of those crosses was symbolized every segment of humanity. On the center cross was Jesus Christ, who died for sin. On the left was a thief who rejected Christ and went to hell. He died in his sins. On the right cross was the thief who died and went to heaven. He died to sin. One died for sin, one died in sin, and one died to sin and was eternally saved. On which side of the cross are you?

The thief on the left did not die and go to hell for what he did. To be sure he was a murderer, a thief, a seditionist, a liar. Probably by every rule of the book he should have gone to hell. But he did not go to hell because he was any of these things. He did not go to hell because of anything that he did, but because of what he did not do. He merely refused to accept the provision that was provided him in Jesus Christ. The Bible says that all have sinned, and the wages of sin is death. We are innately lost. We go from the womb estranged, speaking lies and hypocricies. "Behold I was shapen in iniquity and in sin did my mother conceive me," said David. The very nature of life is of the nature of sin. The thief on the right like every person among us was a sinner. And the wages of sin is death. He did not have to do anything to be lost. He already was lost, because the heart of the desperately wicked, who can know it?

If a doctor were to come to you as you were on your deathbed and say, "When you feel the death gurgle in your throat, when you feel that death is near, if you'll just take this medicine, I promise you that you will live," you would not have to take a knife and plummet it into your breast, nor would you have to take a gun and blow your brains out to die. All you would have to do to die would be to do nothing. Just ignore the medicine. Just reject the offer of life that was given to you. Just don't do anything and you would die.

The thief on the left died in his sin so near to Jesus he could have literally reached out and touched him had his hands not been nailed to the cross. And yet, though he was that close, he refused to accept what had been done for him.

You say, "Preacher, if I had been that near Christ on the cross that day I would have been saved." And yet by the power and presence of the Holy Spirit you are that near today! You are closer to Christ than that man ever was. Yet, though he has been seeking you, you have not opened your heart and reached out to touch him.

But there was still another man on Calvary. The thief on the right. He was converted. I want us for a few minutes to give our attention to the conversion of the thief on the cross.

First of all, it was a wonderful conversion. Did you ever know one that wasn't? I've heard the wonderful conversion stories of many people. I think of the story of Hyman Appleman, a brilliant Jewish lawyer, who came to America at fourteen years of age, unable to speak English, and started in the first grade. And who by the time he was twenty-one had graduated from a university here in the United States and was a brilliant practicing lawyer. I think of the conversion of Stuart Hamblin, who one night in a drunken stupor, sat down and wrote, "I won't go hunting with you, Jake, but I'll go chasing women." And who a few days later was gloriously converted and wrote, "It is no secret what God can do. What he's done for others, he will do for you."

I've seen some outstanding conversions. The word "conversion" literally means with a change, a new style, a new type, a new character, a new personality. A psychologist said to me not long ago, "We can take them apart, but we can't put them together again."

Well, I know a man, and Jesus is his name, who can take you apart and put you back together.

This was a wonderful conversion in many ways. Think of the wonder of it. There was the rebellious crowd on every hand, the carnival atmosphere as three supposed rebels against society were being crucified on the city garbage dump. It was a holiday. They were all there, the barker, the peddlers, the curious, the sarcastic, the unbelieving, and yet this man on his deathbed, as he looked at Jesus Christ a few inches away, dying for the sins of the world, became the first man to enter arm in arm into the gates of glory with the Savior. Redeemed by faith in the blood of Jesus Christ. It was indeed a wonderful conversion.

Two, it was an early conversion. Now you say preacher, "No, you're mistaken. This was a deathbed repentance. And this is a proof text for deathbed repentance." My friend, you are wrong. It did happen to be a deathbed repentance, but this is not the reason this is recorded in the Bible. And this is not the most important thing for us to learn from the text. It is the best case in the Bible for childhood conversion. To be sure, there is one deathbed repentance in the Bible, that none should despair. But only one that none should presume.

Third, it was an immediate conversion. He never joined a church, he was never baptized. He never partook of the Lord's Supper. He was saved on the spot. He said, "Lord, remember me when thou comest into thy kingdom." And Jesus said, "This day shalt thou be with me in paradise." Conversion is not a process of osmosis. You do not just gradually grow into it, because you are in the presence of other converted people. You do not become a Christian because your friends are Christians. Or you are not saved because your parents are Christians. God has no grandchildren! You are a child of God because you have been born into the kingdom of God. Conversion, like a birth, takes place immediately. When a man says yes to Christ, Christ says yes to him. He looked at Jesus and said, "Lord, remember me," and Jesus said, "Today shalt thou be with me in paradise."

Four, it was an open conversion. Tradition has it that there were probably three thousand people around the cross. Think of it. Hundreds and thousands looking on. And yet as he was bleeding and dying on Calvary, Jesus was near to this man, and he was not ashamed of him. He opened his heart before all the world. The Bible over and over again says, "Confess me before men." Jesus says, "Be ashamed of me and I'll be ashamed of you." If this man could have the courage to confess Christ on the cross, you can and must have the courage to walk down this aisle tonight and confess Jesus Christ as your Lord and Savior. The whole world knew! Thousands have been blessed and inspired and saved because of his wonderful testimony.

Five, it was a complete conversion. He didn't just say, "Savior, keep me out of hell. I need a fire insurance policy." No, the Bible records that he cried, "Lord, remember me when thou comest into thy kingdom."

Jesus Christ is called Lord eleven times in the Bible for every time that he is called Savior. It's not enough to make him your Savior. He wants to be and he must be your Lord. It was a complete conversion. He made him the Lord as well as the Savior of his life. God has no bargain basement children. You cannot take the benefits of salvation, without the obligation of salvation. You must make him your Lord and Master as well. It was a complete conversion.

Six, it was a simple conversion. He didn't know a lot of theology. He didn't know anything about the Bible. He had probably never been to church in his life. But he knew one thing, Jesus had what he needed. He had seen his sin and he had seen Christ's provision for sin. He didn't join the church, he didn't know a lot of big words. He didn't take the catechism, he didn't attend several months of a new member's class. How wonderful it was in its simplicity. He merely said, "Lord, remember me when thou comest into thy kingdom."

Seven, it was an abundant conversion. That is, he got more than he expected. More than he had ever hoped for. Listen! "Lord, remember me when thou comest into thy kingdom." He didn't know when Jesus was going to come into his kingdom. He didn't know when he was going to heaven. He didn't know anything about that. He said, "Later on at some future date," so to speak. "By and by, remember me." Jesus said, "I'll beat that. I'll do a whole lot better than that. Today, right now, this very day, thou shalt be with me in paradise." Isn't that just like Jesus. You come to him for whatever needs you have and I promise you that he will do more for you than you could hope or expect or think. What about you? Have you had an experience with God? Conversion is the most wonderful thing in the world.

5

The New Birth

"There was a man of the Pharisees, named Nicodemus, a ruler of the Jews:

"The same came to Jesus by night, and said unto him, Rabbi, we know that thou art a teacher come from God: for no man can do these miracles that thou doest, except God be with him.

"Jesus answered and said unto him, Verily, verily, I say unto thee, Except a man be born again, he cannot see the kingdom of God.

"Nicodemus saith unto him, How can a man be born when he is old? can he enter the second time into his mother's womb, and be born?

"Jesus answered, Verily, verily, I say unto thee, Except a man be born of water and of the Spirit, he cannot enter into the kingdom of God.

"That which is born of the flesh is flesh; and that which is born of the Spirit is spirit.

"Marvel not that I said unto thee, Ye must be born again" (John 3:1-7).

If you were to take all of the world's great religious personalities today, and roll them into one, you would have a man something like Nicodemus. Yet Jesus said to him, "Ye must be born again." Without this dynamic revolutionary mystical experience called new birth, you cannot enter into the kingdom of God.

Now my question to you is simply this: If this man,

this impossibly good man, had to have this new-birth experience to see the kingdom of God, how do you think you and I will get within a million miles of heaven without the same thing? It is life's most important question, "Have you been born again?"

Consider these important facts. First, the new birth is personal. Jesus said, "Ye," or as we would say it, "You." The old spiritual says, "It's not my sister or my brother, but it's me, Oh Lord, standing in the need of prayer," and so it is. Conversion is not a group action. Salvation is not obtained by osmosis. You are not a Christian because you live in a Christian land, belong to a Christian church or were born in a Christian home. Religion is personal; you, yourself, individually, personally must be born again.

If being born in a Christian home made one a Christian, then by the same logic being born in a garage would make you an automobile, or being born in a breadpan would make you a biscuit. Many people think they are Christians because America is a Christian land. But except a man personally be born of the Spirit, except *ye* be born again, except *ye* have a personal experience with God, *ye* shall not enter into the kingdom of heaven.

Secondly, the new birth is imperative. Jesus said, "Ye must!" He did not say, ye may or ye might, if you want to, if it is convenient, or if your denomination believes that way. He said, Ye must. Period. That is it, finished, through, over, terminated, done with. It is the last word on the subject. It doesn't really matter whether you like it or not, whether you believe it or not, or whether you can accept or understand it. The night will always follow day; 2 and 2 will always be 4. *Good men and bad will always have to be born again to enter the kingdom of God.* There is no excuse, there is no short cut or substitute; there is no other way. You must be born again and that is that.

Sincerity will not substitute for accuracy. You say, "But preacher, we are all doing the best we can. We are all sincerely trying to go to the same place." Very true and that's the difference, we are not supposed to be trying at all. Salvation is a finished act. Salvation is not what one does, it is what one has done *for* him. A new creature born again by the Spirit of God, his heart converted, his character changed, his personality transformed, introduced by the Holy Spirit into the kingdom of God.

I once heard of a man who went to his medicine cabinet in the middle of the night and in the darkness took some poison by mistake. He sincerely believed it was medicine. He was very sincere but he was sincerely wrong and the next day he was sincerely dead. You can sincerely believe that $5 + 5 = 11$, but they will always total 10. Sincerity is no substitute for truth. The new birth is imperative, it is not your prerogative to choose between one of many ways. It is the way, the only way. You have to do this; you are constrained to do so. It is required, it is demanded; you must be born again!

Thirdly, the new birth is positive. It is definite. How could anyone miss it? We are naturally in a state of death. We must be drastically changed, made over, born again.

The new birth is a definite act that gains men entrance into the kingdom of God. It is not a patching up of the old personality, nor is it an overhaul of the "Old Man." It is an imparting by the Holy Spirit of an entirely new nature. This is where many people miss it. When we are saved, the old nature is not eradicated; its presence is still there. Its power potentially is rendered impotent. The divinely imparted new nature can prevail, and make victory in the Christian life a reality. The penalty, the consequence of sin is paid. The judgment of the old nature is enacted, we are forgiven, now judged, but still very much with us until we are translated and receive a glorified body, incorruptible, which is not susceptible to the lust of the flesh and the pride of eye.

So now, the born-again child of God has two natures, the new and the old. The sainted apostle says it like this: "When I would do good, evil is continually with me." Hear him as he cries, "Oh, wretched man that I am, who shall deliver me from the vile body of this flesh?" But listen, now the new nature speaks, the born-again Spirit within him now cries in transcendent victory, "Thanks be unto God which giveth us our victory through the Lord Jesus Christ." The apostle Paul, as do all believers, after his new birth experience on the Damascus road now had two natures: The old nature of the flesh and the new nature of the Spirit. The new birth does not patch up the old nature. Men do not put new wine in old wine skins. The new birth gives us a brand new nature, a spiritual nature, a second nature, and now we have two.

Years ago, a famed lawyer said to his pastor, "Sir, would to God that I could be a better man." "'Twould be far easier," replied the minister, "to make you a new man." How true.

The new birth is not reformation. It is not turning over a new leaf, starting again, trying to do better. Suppose at this minute you could so reform as to never sin again. Well and good. That takes care of the future;

no more sins from now on. But what about the sins of the past? What about the sins of yesterday? When a baby is born, it is not 9 months old on its first birthday, it is not one year and 9 months. The fetal period before birth does not count. He is a new being, a new person, life is all in the future. Reformation only takes care of the future. Quitting your sins only takes care of tomorrow. But the new birth takes care of the past, present and future!

A young man in Southern California told me that he had been divorced three times, dishonorably discharged from the Navy, made and lost $700,000, had been kicked out of one university and was flunking out in another. He was only twenty-two years old. "Preacher," he said, "I guess I was just born wrong." "Yes," I replied, "that's right, you were born wrong. We were all born wrong, but you can be right, you can be born again."

Ponce de Leon searched for the fountain of youth, the water of beginning again. Jesus said, I am the water of life, I am that fountain. He that believeth in me shall never die. His body shall die but he will live forever, because the new birth is in the heart.

The social gospelers tried to feed, clothe, house, and control the demoniac from Gadara. But reformation and external improvements were to no avail. They should have known, poor souls, that the myth that man could be saved by his social environment was blown to bits years ago in the Garden of Eden. But when Jesus met the man and entered his heart, by faith, he was born again and the next day they found him, fully clothed and in his right mind, sitting at the feet of Jesus.

The new birth is not a second physical birth. The

very idea is absurd and yet the idea of a new birth was so new to Nicodemus that he really believed Jesus was talking about a second physical birth. "How can a man be born when he is old?" he asked. "Can a man enter a second time into his mother's womb and be born?" Of course not. That which is born of the flesh is only flesh; that which is born of the water is only water; that which is born of the womb is the fruit of the womb, the flesh. For centuries, the doctors have called the physical birth, the water birth. A baby in his mother's womb is entirely encompassed in water. The breaking water announces that birth is on its way. The human child is literally born of the water and in the water. There is no question here of baptism. They are not even remotely discussing it. The controversial fifth verse in which Jesus says a man must be born of the water and of the Spirit is surrounded by a verse on either side which explains that the physical birth of the child from the mother's womb is all that is in question. Baptism is not even in the picture. That which is born of the flesh is flesh and can only produce flesh. No, Nicodemus, you do not need a rebirth of the flesh (a second water birth) but a birth of the Spirit.

A Christian and a Communist were standing on a street corner. A beggar walked by, unshaven, unkept, and poorly clothed. "See that man?" said the Communist. "There is your Capitalism. If Communism were in power, Communism would put a new suit of clothes on that man's back." "If Jesus Christ were in power in that man's life," replied the Christian, "Jesus would put a new man in that suit of clothes." That is conversion, that is the new birth. That is the difference.

We say that a man has a soul. But technically a man is a soul that has a body. The soul, the heart, the character, the ego, the id, the will, the personality; that is the man. That is where we live, that is what must be changed. The body is only the decaying tabernacle in which man lives. Science tells us that every seven years man undergoes a complete biological organic change and no portion of your body is the same as it was seven years before. If the body were the man, then every life termer would have to be released from prison after seven years, because the man that went into the penitentiary is not there anymore. The body is not the man. The heart is the man, and that is what must be born again.

The new birth is not a second physical birth. Baptism is not the new birth. Baptism is a picture of the new birth; it signifies the fact that the old corrupt nature is dead and buried and that one is now possessed with a new nature, a resurrected nature, that lives and that has been born again. Church membership is not the new birth. To be sure, it is commanded for the born-again Christian, but like baptism, it is *because* of salvation; not in order to *obtain* salvation. The card one signs and the pencil with which one writes in applying for church membership only touches the hand, but the new birth takes place in the heart. Membership in a Christian church does not make me a Christian anymore than joining the Girl Scouts would make me a girl. Church membership is for people who have experienced the new birth and who are joining with others who have had a similar experience and are trying to share it with the lost.

To obtain the new birth, to understand it in its fulness, is something that can never be described. It must be experienced. How can you explain the taste of ice cream to one with no sense of taste? Who can describe a beautiful rose to a blind man? It cannot be described; it only can be experienced.

Do you want to experience the new birth? Then you are well on your way to doing so, for the first step is desire. You must want it more than anything in the world. If you are satisfied to live a Christless life, only touching the hem of the garment of real living and then spend a Godless eternity—you can never be saved. He will never come into your heart against your will. You must WANT to be born again.

Secondly, you must submit yourself to the will of God and the lordship of Jesus Christ. Often times people say to me, "Will I have to give up smoking or dancing or drinking to be saved?" I do not know whether you will have to give up wearing green socks or eating asparagus, but you must be willing to give up everything. You don't come to Jesus Christ on your terms. There must be an absolute abandonment of your will to the will of God. Do not fear; it is not that he might do you ill, but only that he can do you good.

A surgeon asks your complete surrender to him only for your own good that he might impart life and healing into your body. Jesus Christ wants your will for your good. He needs none of your help, your instruction; he is the master surgeon. He is most capable of performing the surgery of the new birth. Willingly, you must yield—freely, you must submit; allowing him to do any and everything that he deems necessary in engrafting his new nature into your personality.

Third, there must be repentance. Ask him to cleanse and forgive your sin, that basic rebellious nature that has set your will against his for years. To repent is to confess your sins to God, tell him you are sorry of it. To feel sorry, to be sorry and to quit doing it with his help; setting your mind in the direction of God rather than away from God.

Fourth, there must be faith. He has never lied and he will not lie to you now. I can lie; others may lie; your best friend may lie; but not Jesus. He says, "I stand at the door of your heart. I want to come in and I will come in if you will but ask me to."

It is no accident that the Spirit of God has brought you to this place to join with these thousands in hearing this message. You cannot hide, you cannot run away from God, you can never again say you did not know. There is no way out; you have no excuse. You look to the left, there are your sins; look to the right, there are your transgressions. Look to the past; there are your failures of yesterday. Look to the future; there are the continued frustrations of tomorrow. Look beneath; there are the yawning jaws of hell, expanding to engulf you in the penitentiary of the damned. Where will you go? Which way can you turn? What will you do? The answer? Look up! Look up! By two moves, the move of repentance of sin and the secondary move of faith in Jesus Christ, you can win the game of life! You *can* be born again. You *must* be born again. *You* may be born again. You *will* be born again, if you will turn in repentance to God and in faith ask Jesus Christ to come into your heart. Do it now. Do it now. Ye must be born again!

6

Five Fearful Facts from the Bible

In Matthew 7:13 the speaker is the great authority, Jesus Christ himself. "Enter ye in at the straight gate; for wide is the gate, and broad is the way, that leadeth to destruction, and many there be which go in thereat: Because straight is the gate, and narrow is the way, which leadeth unto life, and few there be that find it.

"Beware of false prophets, which come to you in sheep's clothing, but inwardly they are ravening wolves.

"Ye shall know them by their fruits. Do men gather grapes of thorns. or figs of thistles?

"Even so every good tree bringeth forth good fruit; but a corrupt tree bringeth forth evil fruit.

"A good tree cannot bring forth evil fruit, neither can a corrupt tree bring forth good fruit.

"Every tree that bringeth not forth good fruit is hewn down, and cast into the fire.

"Wherefore by their fruits ye shall know them.

"Not everyone that saith unto me, Lord, Lord, shall enter into the kingdom of heaven; but he that doeth the will of my Father which is in heaven.

"Many will say to me in that day, Lord, Lord, have we not prophesied in thy name? and in thy name have cast out devils? and in thy name done many wonderful works?

"And then will I profess unto them, I never

knew you, depart from me, ye that work iniquity"
(vv. 14-23).

The Bible is a very frank book, recording both the
sins and the successes of the saints. The gospel is a
two-edged sword. It speaks of salvation, but also of
damnation. It speaks of salvation, but it also speaks of
perdition. It speaks of heaven, but it talks of hell. The
Bible over and over again presents both sides of life.
The Word of God is a wonderful positive book, and
every preacher in the world prefers to preach on the
positive side of the gospel. The word "gospel" actually
has nothing but a positive side, for it means good news.
The fact that men are going to hell is not good news.
The fact that the wages of sin is death is not good news.
And although these negative aspects of the Scriptures
are not strictly a part of the good news gospel, they
are a part of the teachings of Christ which break up the
fallow ground, stir the hearts of men, and make them
receptive and susceptible to the gospel. Now, I know
that we would rather think about positive things, and
I would rather preach about them; but our generation
needs to be reminded that there is a judgment to shun,
that there are some negative aspects of the gospel. The
wages of sin is death and it's not all honeymoon and
roses in the Word of God.

The Bible promises many wonderful positive things.
It says, "In the beginning was the Word, and the Word
was with God, and the Word was God." I like that.
"The Lord is my shepherd, I shall not want." "He that
believeth on me, these works that I do, shall he do and
greater works." "I am the resurrection and the life: he
that believeth in me, though he were dead, yet shall
he live." "If ye abide in me, and my words abide in
you, ye shall ask what ye will, and it shall be done unto

you." "As many as received him, to them gave he the power to become the sons of God." "And we know all things work together for good to them that love God." "And whosoever shall call upon the name of the Lord shall be saved." "For with God all things are possible." Where shall we stop? The Bible is a wonderfully positive book. But let us not forget that while it is the judgment of God that breaks the stony hearts of men, it is the sweet river of God's love that flows it into salvation. And yet, the two-pronged hammer, the two-edged sword, the two-sided message of the Scripture has both a negative and a positive side. Now, I want to remind us against the backdrop of a society in which anything goes, and everything is lollypop and roses, that tends to lull ourselves into a positive philosophy, that there are some negative aspects of the Word of God.

I remind you briefly and simply tonight of but five of them. We have read them in our Scriptures. They are the five fearful facts from the faithful Word of God.

One, not everyone is going to be saved. Let it be soundly remembered that the pronouncement of Scripture is that some go to hell, while some go to heaven. Some are saved, while some are damned. I think that if we would be honest with ourselves, the lack of missionary zeal, the lack of evangelistic fervor in all of us, basically results from the idea in most of our hearts that really if the truth were known that we all think that some day we'll wake up to find that, after all, a good God wouldn't send anybody to hell, and after all most folks are good folks. If we would be honest, we would acknowledge that we really do, most of us, believe in the Fatherhood of God, and the brotherhood of man.

Every once in a while all the Jews, and Catholics,

and Protestants get together and all have a big Christian brotherhood day. They reason thusly: God is the father of us all, he made us all. True, but he also made the skunk, and the buzzard, and the rattlesnake, and they're not sons of God. Jesus said of some of the most religious people that ever lived, "You are of your father the devil." Jesus said enter into the straight gate.

Let it get firmly entrenched in our minds and hearts tonight, some people in this auditorium will spend eternity in hell. That husband into whose face you look across the breakfast table every morning, that child to whom you have not witnessed. That neighbor you've never tried to win to Christ, and some of you yourselves are on the way to hell! But do we really believe it? We find it hard to grasp. And we all hope against hope that someday we'll wake up to find it was all one big theological fairy story, and God just winks at us, and though it makes him sad to see the way we live, he'll always say, "I forgive." Most people have the idea that God is a kind of religious computer, a sort of spiritual Santa Claus that sits up in heaven and frowns every time we do something wrong. But though he doesn't like it, though he doesn't like our blasphemy and our adultery, our stealing his money, and desecrating his day, or wasting our opportunities and blaspheming his Word, He just grins at it and says, "Well, that's all right, I understand. You did the best you could. You were sincere. Come on, let's all go to heaven anyway!"

It is a lie! It is not true! Let it be clearly implanted in our minds that Jesus Christ came from the portals of heaven to die on the old rugged cross, to keep men out of hell because some are going to hell. And only a few are going to heaven. Fact number one, fearful, awesome, penetrating from the Word of God, not everyone is going to be saved.

The second fearful fact from the Word of God is this. More will be lost than will be saved. Now listen again. "Enter into the straight gate, for narrow is the way that leadeth to everlasting life, and few there be that find it. But broad is the way that leadeth to destruction, and many there be that go in thereat." Not only are some lost and going to hell, while some go to heaven, but more will go to hell than will go to heaven. Now that too is hard to believe. Could Jesus really mean that? When he said broad is the way and many there be that go in thereat? But very few there are that enter in at the straight gate. Did he really mean that? Or was he just speaking symbolically?

Now, preacher, I can understand that some folks would go to hell. Surely, the outcast, the prostitute, the pimp, the pervert, the purveyor of flesh, the peddler of smut, the dope addict, the discard, the reject, the rebel, the leftovers from the one-way street of life; surely, they're going to hell. But preacher, after all, aren't most folks good folks? Yes, they are. I've found that to be true. Most people are good people. So? So, what? You say, "Well, doesn't that mean that most folks will go to heaven?" Now, wait a minute, you didn't understand the Scripture. You might as well say, "Preacher, don't you think the Yankees will win the pennant this year, because, after all, doesn't our church have a good music program?" Yes, we have. So, what? What you are talking about, however, has absolutely nothing to do with each other. Yes, most folks are good folks. But good folks do not go to heaven. And bad folks do not go to hell.

The Bible says all have sinned, all have missed the

maik. All have come short of the glory of God. We have turned, everyone, to his own way, behold we are all shapen in iniquity.

No matter how good men are they cannot be good enough to save themselves. For by grace are ye saved, through faith, and that not of yourselves. It is the gift of God, not of works, lest any man should boast.

Most folks are good folks. But the only thing that determines hell or heaven, salvation or damnation, is this. If you have ever sinned one sin in all your life, you cannot atone for that sin and that sin makes you lost. Whether it is one or a million you're lost and separated from God, and only Jesus Christ in his perfection can make you saved. Unless you've been born again by faith in the blood of Jesus Christ, unless your heart has been made whole and new by an encounter with Christ, a personal experience with God in which life-giving power came into your life from his life, you are lost, and separated from God.

More will be lost than will be saved, because most people go about trying to establish their own righteousness. "I've joined the church, I've been baptized, I've been good, I've given to the church, I'm a good citizen, I've done all of these things." But they have missed faith in Jesus Christ. The good people don't go to heaven. Those go to heaven who have been born again and have faith in Jesus Christ. The bad people do not go to hell. Those go to hell who have never received Christ as their personal Savior. And the world is filled with works religion. Do this, do that, do something else. But Jesus Christ spells religion this way, d-o-n-e. Not d-o. It is done, it is finished. He did it all on the cross. The minority are saved. The majority are lost.

The third fearful fact from the Bible is this. And I

think that it is the most awful and awesome one of them all. Many people expecting to be saved, will be lost. How awful to join a church, to give to the campfire girls, to help little old ladies across the street, to vote in every election, to partake of every church ordinance, to be confirmed, to be baptized at First Church and still expecting to be saved, fool and deceive yourself to die and go to hell. Many expecting to be saved will be lost. Look, "Then will I say unto them, depart. I never knew you. Depart from me ye that work iniquity." No matter how good you work, all of your works are evil, and even your good deeds iniquitous, unless something has happened. What is it? It's in the same verse. "I never knew you." He will say, "Depart from me you that work iniquity." In other words, those who will be lost expecting to be saved, will be those who never knew Christ. Do you remember in the Old Testament when the Bible says that Adam knew his wife and she conceived and bore a child? Lot and Cain and Abel knew their wives and they conceived. Mary discovering she was of child with the Holy Ghost said, "How can these things be, being I know not a man?" Jesus said, "Depart from me, I never knew you." It simply means to be in oneness with him. The twain becoming one, that's Christ in you, that's you, if any man be in Christ, becoming a new creature.

When a man and a woman are married, they have one name, one family, one bank account, one home, one. To know someone is to be in union with him. Jesus is saying that many people who joined the church, who counted their beads, who had an emotional experience, who did all these things, are lost, because they never joined him—never knew him. It means exactly what you think it does. It means to be in oneness with.

Ladies and gentlemen, listen very closely. Don't deceive yourselves. If you had a genuine transforming experience in God in faith and have Christ in your heart, the kind that saves you, when the twain become one, you now have his personality. You now have his desires. You now have his heart. You now have his life. You now do what he does. And if you habitually find it impossible to give, detest to go to church, do not enjoy the preaching of the gospel, will not follow Christ in baptism, refuse to join the church, take no delight in the reading of the Word of God, then you are none of his. If Christ is in you, his works will you do. He will live in you.

Now listen. You came down an aisle. The preacher asked you some questions. Then you nodded your head and sat down. You filled out a card. You were immersed. And yet you go to the same places, you act the same way. Church is still a drag and religion is still nothing. You still love to be out there in the world. You think you are going to die and go to heaven and hocus-pocus you're going to praise God, and love Jesus and enjoy the fellowship of the saints throughout eternity. Oh, no. You wouldn't be in heaven five minutes before you would be asking how to get out. You'd be miserable. The Bible says, "Outside the gate, outside are those, the whoremongers, the liars, the thief, the adulterer, whosoever loveth and maketh a lie; inside the gate are those who have his nature." You come to church, the music is professional, the preaching is short, the sanctuary is commodious, the seats are soft. And yet you are miserable. You don't enjoy it. You feel foreign to it. You do not have the nature of it. Its witness does not bear witness with your spirit. You wind your watch, and the hours are interminable. You think you are going to heaven? You think you have the nature of Christ? You think he lives in you? You think you know him? Oh, if you had been playing golf or watching a ballgame, or fishing, or going to the show, the hours would have sailed by. "Then will I say to many, I never knew you." Be not deceived!

I want you to take inventory. If any man have not the spirit of Christ, he is none of his. Friend, when the old time religion hits you, when the Spirit of God comes into your life, you can't help but do what he wants you to do. When I was saved, I couldn't get in that water fast enough. When I was married, I couldn't put on the ring quickly enough. I wanted everyone to know I had a wonderful wife. I wanted everybody to know I was a Christian. Those who must be plotted against and prodded and encouraged and pushed and cajoled into doing the will of God by constraint rather than by willingness, certainly do not know Christ. They are not in oneness with him.

Not everyone will be saved. More will be lost than will be saved. Many expecting to be saved will be lost. Don't deceive yourself.

And the fourth fearful fact from the Bible is this. There will be no one saved after death. I'm not riding the Catholics tonight. If I ever get the Baptists straightened out, I'll go to work on the Catholics. But I'm saying to you, that we Baptists, if we told the truth, really believe in a kind of Baptist purgatory. Most of us do not believe that it is all settled right here and now. But that God is a kind of cross-section between Emily Post and Santa Claus who sits up there and every time we pull a no-no, he puts a minus over hero on the other side. And God just waits and watches and when we all get to judgment, he adds them all up, and he is the most surprised of all as to whether we go to heaven or to hell!

Now we really think that. A man said to me, "We'll never know whether we made it or not until we get there. I'm doing the best that I can. Pray for me that I hold out faithful. I'm just hoping that I've done more good deeds than bad deeds. And we won't know until then, whether we are saved or not!"

When I was in high school, I didn't always do as well as I could. I enjoyed high school, though. As a matter of fact I spent three of the happiest years of my life as a sophomore in high school. But when that teacher came along and said, "You passed," I didn't have any question as to what she was talking about. The Bible says that when we receive Christ we are passed from death unto life. The Bible does not say we are going to pass, but that we have *already* passed! We are not going to be saved, we have been saved.

You're not going to determine after death, whether you are saved or not. The Son of Man has power on earth to forgive sins. God operates here and now in this life. He doesn't have the power to save you in the next life. His power is operative in this earth, now, in this life, in this day, this opportunity. What you do with Jesus and whether you receive him and his life-giving power to make you a child of God, will determine whether you go to hell or to heaven. It's not going to be determined later on.

The fifth fearful fact from the Word of God and the final one is this: This could be your last night, your last chance to be saved. I've conducted funerals for nine-year-old boys, as well as for eighty-nine-year-old men. Ladies and gentlemen, listen to me! Because of drugs and sedatives and knockout drugs to ease the pain, not one out of fifty dies conscious these days. They die unconscious. Deathbed repentances are few and far between. I am conscious that every time I stand to preach someone here may be dead by tomorrow morning. You say preacher, don't try to scare me, don't talk to me about death. All right! You promise me you'll never die, and I'll promise you I won't talk about death.

There's nothing more beautiful in all the world than a sea of faces, but what's at the end of it, a hole in the ground. Death comes to us all! It could come to you in the next five seconds. This could be your last night to be saved. And what if it were?

Hyman Appleman was preaching a revival in the high school auditorium sponsored by the churches of the city. It was about 1939 or '40, just before the beginning of the war. He said that night after night as he preached six thugs came to hear him. They sat in the furtherest corner of the balcony. He would tell a joke, and they would go "Ha, Ha, Ha." He preached and they would say, "Aaaaaamen!" They'd bring a whiskey bottle and while he was preaching they'd go pop, pop, pop by sticking their finger in it, all through the service. Hyman said he did his best to talk to them. They smarted off and wouldn't budge.

One day one of the six was killed in an accident, crossing a street going to school, in front of hundreds of students during the revival. The other five boys were five of the six pallbearers.

They didn't come to the revival that night or the next. But on the third night two of them returned. And one of them, the leader of the crowd, was the first one down the aisle. He said that as he came down to the front, Hyman thinking that he had come to cause trouble and laugh and ridicule, pulled him to one side and stuck him behind the piano and said, "If you've come down here to make more trouble, so help me I'll . . . " The boy pushed the preacher's hand down and said, "Preacher, have a heart, can't a guy change his mind?" Hyman said, "All right, but what have you come for?" He answered, "I want to be saved." And he was! And Dr. Appleman said after it was over, he talked to him and said, "You were so smart, you were so arrogant, so rebellious, what made the difference?" He said, "Preacher, I could laugh at your sermons, I could laugh at your jokes, I could ridicule your funny stories, I could hee-haw your swinging arms, I could make fun of your accent, but there's nothing funny about an open grave."

Ladies and gentlemen, you are going to die. Whether you spend eternity in hell or heaven will be determined for many of you by what you do this night in this invitation for Jesus Christ. Death is certain. It could come for you tonight. I have seen at least one man die in church. For Jesus' sake, for your soul's sake, come.

7

Hell

Jesus Christ was the Master Teacher. He was the great storyteller, and he knows what every good teacher knows, the importance of giving vivid illustration to literal truths.

Most people believe that this is one such illustration (Luke 16:19-31). A parable, a made-up story, not a true story, a made-up story to illustrate a truth.

I do not believe that it is a parable. I believe that it is a true story, because Jesus never used a proper name in a parable. And he said there was a certain man named Lazarus. The literal, grammatical construction of the sentence is this, There was a certain man, Lazarus, by name. It is as though Jesus with a double emphasis went to great difficulty to make extra certain that we understood that this was not a parable, but a true story about real people. Now if there was not a man named Lazarus when Jesus said that there was, then he lied. And he could not be my Savior. But nothing could be farther from the truth.

Jesus tells this story, the story of a very rich man. The rich man went to hell, not because he was rich, but because he did not have personal saving faith in Jesus Christ. There is nothing wrong with my being rich. To the contrary, the Bible says that it is God that giveth thee the power to get wealth. And if you make it honestly, and use it for the glory of God, you may thank God every day for the gift of salesmanship or executive ability or whatever it may be that God has given you that gives you the power to get wealth.

Now, by the same token, the poor man did not go to heaven just because he was poor and God wanted to reward the poor people. He went to heaven because he was a child of God. Because he had been saved, because he had faith in the living Christ.

The Bible tells us that the state of these two men was vastly different, in this life and in the next.

One can almost hear the shuffling of the hoofs of the thoroughbred horses yonder in the stable. The running to and fro of the servants who waited on the every beck and call of the rich man. The finest sherbet from Egypt, caviar and quail on toast was served every day as he lay upon his couch in finely-starched linen shirts. And with the mere flick of his wrist people came to wait upon his every need.

He was not an especially bad man. The Bible tells us that outside of his gates a beggar was allowed to live. What a good place for a beggar to be, for as his rich friends came in, they would give him money. The Bible says that he lived on the residue, the leftover from the table of bounty and plenty from the rich man. And so this rich man was probably a very good man. The Bible tells us that he was clothed in purple and fine linen. Purple is a sign of royalty in the Word of God. One who was a king or a prince, in Jesus' day, as the political leader, was also the religious leader of his people. So, he was not only a very rich man, a very famous and prosperous man, he was also probably a very religious man. Religious on the outside. But one day he died. I can imagine that the headlines of the Jerusalem Gazette must have heralded the news, that a very rich and prominent citizen had passed on. Perhaps they had come from far and near, bedecking his casket with all the tapestries of dignity. The flowers must have been piled high at the graveside. Notables came from far and near to give their last respects to a good and influential civic leader. But what they did not know was that regardless of his riches, his possessions, and affluence, he was lost. And the Bible says that as soon as Jesus Christ finishes telling the story of the death of the rich man, the very next words that he says were, "and in hell." The man was lost.

Now, outside of his gates was a poor man. He was so impoverished that his only friends were the animals. His only food was the leftovers from the rich man's table. I can imagine that one day one of his friends came in and said, "Dives, old Lazarus outside of your gates there seems to be asleep later than usual this morning." They probably went out and looked at him and kicked him and rolled him over, and found him to be dead. Perhaps they waited until the trash collectors came. Perhaps he didn't even have a decent burial. Perhaps they rang a golden bell and someone came from in back of the servant's quarters to give him a burial on the outskirts of town where the paupers were buried in countless nameless graves.

But the Bible tells us that this poor man went to heaven. And the only thing that reversed their circumstances in life, the only thing that made a difference is that one man had an experience with God. One man was looking by faith to trust the only Savior that could save a man's soul.

In hell, the rich man learned some things. I want us to profit from his experience. In hell he learned four things, from which we can profit. Too late for himself, but may God be pleased, not too late for you.

One, he learned the certainty of hell. Now intelligent people have always asked the question is there really a hell. I believe that there is. I believe it for many reasons. I believe it because the college I attended taught me to believe it. I believe it because the seminary I attended taught me to believe it. I believe it because the preachers of all time that God has used to mightily win nations to God and bring multitudes to Christ have all believed the Word of God at the point of hell. I believe in hell, because my denomination teaches it. I believe it because today's preachers in whom I have confidence believe in the reality of hell. But I believe in hell for many other reasons. I believe in it because of the multitude of times with which the Bible refers to a literal hell. Did you know that the Bible says more about hell than it does about heaven, the Lord's Supper, and baptism all rolled into one? Over and over again God warns men to repent and says the wages of sin is death and whosoever was not found written in the book of life was cast into the lake of fire.

People say to me, "Don't try to scare me. Give me the positive side of the gospel." To be sure the gospel does have a positive side. But I warn you that the two-sided edge of the sword of the gospel has a positive side, but it does have a negative side as well. Some people say that's no reason to be saved. But frankly, I don't think it is particularly a sign of one's superior intelligence to say I don't want to step out in front of a train because I just want to go on living. I think it is also a pretty good sign if one doesn't want to get killed. I don't think it is particularly a sign of one's superior intellectualism to say I don't want to be saved just because I don't want to go to hell. Frankly, I think it's pretty smart not to want to go to hell. I think it's one of the smartest decisions you will ever make in your life. I know that to be saved is to have heaven on earth. I know that it means you'll go to heaven when you die. I know that the Christian is better in this life even if there were no eternity. But I also believe that it makes good sense for a man to use his mentality and realize that to be a Christian means to miss some things as well as to gain some things. I don't think you are very smart to want to get cancer or to get run over by a truck. And wanting to miss hell is not a particularly bad motivation for being saved. As a matter of fact I think it makes pretty good sense!

I believe in hell because the disciples taught it. The apostles believed it. And I believe in hell more than any reason because the greatest gentlemen who ever lived, he who cannot lie, he who must tell the truth because he is the truth incarnate in human flesh, Jesus Christ, himself, said, "and in hell."

Secondly, he found out about the character of hell. What kind of place is it? Ladies and gentlemen, I believe that heaven is a place where we will continue to do the wonderful good things of life. But our capacity to enjoy them will be increased manifold a thousand times. We know our loved ones here; we will know them there. We sing here; we shall sing there. But heaven will be a cessation of evil things. Hell will be exactly the opposite. Hell will be a cessation of everything good. And a continuation of everything unpleasant, but magnified in its intensity.

What kind of place is hell? It's a place of life. The

man wasn't dead, he was alive. It's a place where the thirsts and appetites of life continue. He was thirsty in hell. Tell me how much water a man can hold on the tip of his finger. And yet the Bible says it would have been a taste of paradise to the rich man in hell. The thirsty will still thirst. Those who lust will still lust. The adulterer will still burn with passion. The whoremonger will still rage as his blood races with the wind. The drunken will still crave drinks; the dope addict will still crave his dope, but in hell their desires will be magnified and intensified a million fold in their intensity. It's a place of unsatisfied passions, it's a place of no exit, it's a place of endlessness. It is a place of unanswered prayers.

Now I know whether they say it or not, that when people ask the question, "Tell me about the character of hell, what is it really like?" I know what they mean. "Is hell real flame?" I don't know. But I'll tell you something a whole lot better than that. I'm never going to find out!

Let's just pretend for a moment that hell is not real fire. Over and over again the Bible speaks of the flame, the fire of hell. Now, I believe that God knows how to use language. Why don't we question him when he says water? Why don't we question him when he says heaven? Why don't we question him when he says gold? When he says blue, we believe that he means blue. Why do we question that fire means fire? Because we are trying to hope against hope that we can make it easier for ourselves.

All right, let's play that game. Let's pretend that it is symbolic. Suppose you were Jesus Christ, and you were trying to get across to people how awful eternal separation from God is, how would you describe it?

Having no way to describe, no grammatical vehicle by which he could convey to us the way that hell really is, he uses symbolic language. Now, if that is the case, let me ask you this. If flame on the human body was the worst thing that we could comprehend, and he only uses that as descriptive of the real thing, then I want you to tell me what the real thing is like. If that's only symbolic, you haven't made it better, you've made it worse.

Where is hell? Let me ask you a question tonight. Are you sure that hell is in the center of the earth? I don't know. Do you know that hell could be in outer space? The Bible says in hell men fall into a bottomless pit. Now wait a minute. Where else could men fall and keep on falling and never stop? The Bible says that hell is a place of outer darkness. Absolute black empty vastness. Could that be outer space? I do not know, but could it be?

The Bible says that when we confess our sins he forgives them and he puts them as far behind him as the east is from the west. If unforgiven sins are as far as the east is from the west, then the sins that God hates the most and are not forgiven, how far away from God are they? Hell, wherever it is and whatever it is, is a place of absolute and eternal separation from God. You say God's not bad. No, he isn't. He sent his Son to bleed and die in ignominious shame and death on a cross. You're not fair. Tell me what more he could do. What Jesus has done is to make you a free moral agent. He has given you the privilege of choice and you can accept to follow him and his will. And if you will you will follow him right into heaven. But if you reject him and go against God, all he does is to merely abide by your decision and let you go on away from him into the next life.

Hell is a place of absolute, endless, eternal separation from God. Don't go out of here and say that preacher said hell was in outer space. I didn't say that. I simply raise the question of the possibility. I do know this. Hell is just like you have lived on this earth, separated from God!

Third, he found out about the crowd going to hell. You say, "Preacher, what kind of folks go to hell?" Turn over to Revelation 21:8. "But the fearful, and unbelieving, the abominable, and murderers, and whoremongers, and sorcerers, and idolaters, and all liars all have their part in the lake which burneth with fire and brimstone: which is the second death." Now, you say preacher I can understand that the discards and the rejects of life; I can understand the whoremongers and the drunks, the liars, and the thieves will be in hell; but aren't most folks good folks? Do you know what the Bible calls most good folks who have simply not committed their lives to Christ? And had an experience of salvation with Jesus Christ? The Bible calls them unbelievers. Listen again! "But the fearful, and the unbelieving, and the abominable, and the murderer, and the whoremongers," all categorized together. You say, "I'm not an idolater." But you are an unbeliever. "I'm no whoremonger." But you are an unbeliever. "I'm no adulterer." But you are an unbeliever. "I'm no liar." But you are an unbeliever.

The crowd going to hell is the good, the bad, the indifferent, the Methodist, the Presbyterian, the Baptist, the Catholic, no matter who they may be, who have never had an experience of conversion by a committal to Jesus. You say, I believe in him. I can say I believe in that chair, but it is not holding me up. I believe in it, but I have not believed on it until I commit myself to it, and trust it to hold me up. You say I believe in Jesus intellectually. I believe that he lived. You can say you believe that this girl will make a good wife, but until you say, "I do," she does not become yours. You must receive her in faith.

Salvation is not an intellectual belief in the historicity of Jesus Christ. But it is believing on him. It is committing yourself to him, a definite time-and-place experience, where you say an eternal "I do" to Jesus Christ. That's what it means to believe on the Son of God, to give yourself to him, to become a New Testament believer.

Now fourth, he found out about the cross, too late for him, but not too late for you, the cross that would have kept him from hell. Had he heard about it? I can't help but believe that that same prophet of good news, that same preacher of the gospel that came by one day to cause the poor man to be saved, must have been overheard by the rich man. I cannot but believe that he had been exposed to it. But he never did respond. How awful for a man to drown five feet from shore. How awful for one to die just a few seconds before they were able to save his life. He looked into heaven; he saw the cross that spanned the earth; he saw the distance between God and man, that great gulf beyond which no man can go. But he knew too late for himself that his friend was there and he was not.

I believe that the Bible implies that the saved will not be able to know about the misery in hell. But oh, one of the awfullest teachings of the Word of God is that those in hell will see into heaven and will know what they are missing.

Many years ago Gypsy Smith, the great preacher, told the story of how a group of little gypsy travelers were crossing a bridge one day. You may remember how in the army they taught you to break cadence so that when you were crossing a bridge the rhythm would not break it down. They did not do that, and the perpetual clank, clank, of the turning wheels and the horses and the men marching caused the little bridge to give way. With rare presence of mind, seeing the swelling waters beneath, one gypsy boy grabbed his little mother, threw her into the water, away and aside from the crashing horses and chariots that were falling in, and dove in under her to pull her to safety. And out of her head and hysterical as people get, she fought and he had to let her go. Down he went to get her the second and the third time. He did all he could in his young manhood, but the current was too strong, and her resistance too much; and he had to let her go.

Gypsy Smith said two days later they had a mass funeral and buried seven gypsies in an open grave. They tried to restrain him, but when the boy came by, he slipped into that hole in the ground and raising the body of his dead mother, began to weep, "Why didn't you let me, Mama, I could have saved you? I wanted to save you. Why didn't you let me? Why did you fight me?"

Now, I don't believe that when we stand before God in judgment he is going to laugh and say, "I told you you would go to hell!" No, no. I believe he will show you the riven side, the pierced feet, the nail-scarred hands. I believe a tear will glisten on his cheek as he says, "Oh, sinner, why didn't you come that night?

Why didn't you let me? I would have saved you!"

He found out too late about that cross that would have saved him. But you can be saved tonight. Put your faith not in the cross, but in the man who died on the cross. He's been into death; he's been into hell; he's been into the grave. He's conquered. He's built a bridge across hell to the glory land, by which all who come by faith may pass. Receive him. My parting message to you and earnest plea is "Come." Say, "Pastor, I want to receive Jesus by faith. I want him as Lord. I want to put my trust in Christ. I give him my all."

8

The Love of God

"And as Moses lifted up the serpent in the wilderness, even so must the Son of man be lifted up: That whosoever believeth in him should not perish, but have eternal life.

"For God so loved the world, that he gave his only begotten Son, that whosoever believeth in him should not perish, but have everlasting life.

"For God sent not his Son into the world to condemn the world; but that the world through him might be saved.

"He that believed on him is not condemned; but he that believeth not is condemned already, because he hath not believed in the name of the only begotten Son of God" (John 3:14-18).

The love of God is absolutely indescribable. It is undeservable; it is unquenchable; it is unattainable; and it is inexhaustible; and the love of God was, of course, inevitable.

First of all the love of God is indescribable. I feel like a bush leaguer up to bat at Yankee stadium for the first time, when I address myself to the subject of the love of God. I feel completely out of my league, vastly overwhelmed, immensely incapable of even discussing with an intelligent audience the depth of the all-inclusive love of God revealed in Jesus Christ.

What do you think is the biggest word in the Bible?

Is it "Whithersoever," Nebuchadnezzar, or one of those other Old Testament names? I don't think so. I think it is a little two letter word S-O, "So." How big is the love of God? I think that's the biggest word in the world. God SO loved. How much was "so"? How many worlds did God take into his arms? How many sins did he forgive? How many people did he love? How many lives did he invision saving and changing and blessing when he sent his Son on the cross to die because God SO loved the world?

It has been the theme of every writer, the song of every singer. More has been said about it, more has been preached about it, than any other subject in all of Christendom. The indescribable love of God.

God, the greatest being; so loved, the greatest emotion; the world, the greatest possible number of people; that he gave, the greatest sacrifice; his only begotten Son, the greatest possession; that whosoever, the greatest invitation; believeth in him, the greatest plan of salvation; should not perish, the greatest damnation; but have everlasting life, the greatest possession.

What can I say to get across to you the unfathomable depths of God's love? The emotion, the joy unspeakable, and full of glory, the peace of mind, the calmness of spirit, the fulfilment of heart, the newness of life, that is experienced when a man opens his heart to Jesus Christ. The love of God must be experienced, or you will never know its indescribable beauty and power.

Secondly, the love of God is unquenchable. It is not something of which you can merely speak, or sing, although it will be sung and spoken when you have experienced it. The love of God is something that must HAPPEN! The fact that Jesus Christ died on the cross for you, the fact that a carpenter from Nazareth was nailed to two pieces of wood on the city garbage dump two thousand years ago is no more than a historical fact from the archives of history until you have experienced it. The love of God cannot be quenched, it must be experienced. It is something more than a cold historical fact that comes to your heart and knocks at its door. And as friends invite you to church and tell of what Christ means to them, and what he has done for their life, it must be something more than a black sermon on a white piece of paper. But it is nothing more than a historical tragedy unless you open your heart and experience his love and let him come in; and in return give your love to Christ. For when you quench it, when you refuse to open the door of your heart, as God loves you and wants you to do, then you will never be able to experience and truly know what it is all about. How can one describe the beauty of a sunset to a blind man, or the gorgeous strains of a symphony to one that is deaf, or the taste of a prime piece of meat to one who has not the sense of taste?

The love of God cannot be quenched. You must give your heart to him in return or it will be nothing to you —nothing but a cold historical fact.

Thirdly, the love of God is unattainable. It cannot be striven for, it cannot be worked for, it cannot be attained—only obtained. God loves man in his sin. He loves us as we are. It is not something that we can clean ourselves up and get in a position to be worthy of receiving. Christ receiveth sinful man. Even me with all my sins!

The songwriter has said, "What the world needs now is love, sweet love." What the world has now is love. The love that flows from Calvary, the love of God revealed in Christ when God loved the world as no man has ever loved, when Jesus Christ spread-eagled on the cross, made himself of no reputation, and emptied himself for the sins of the world, because God loves you.

People say to me, "I'm too bad to be saved. I'm too mean to be a Christian. I've too many sins to be converted." That's why he wants you to be converted. That's why you need to be saved. That's what it means to open your heart. Not because you are good but because you are bad. It cannot be obtained. For by grace are ye saved through faith, and that not of yourselves, it is the gift of God. Not of works lest any man should boast. If you work for something, it is no longer a gift. It cannot be deserved, it cannot be merited. By grace are ye saved, unmerited favor. God in Christ, doing for us not only what we could not deserve, but also what we could not do for ourselves, and did not even deserve to have done.

People say to me, "I'll quit my sins." "I'll become good enough. I'll come to the place that I'm all right, I'll clean myself up." But if you could, I've got bad news for you. If you could get to the place that you would never sin, if you could clean up your life, if you could quit your sins, and come to God and say, "Now, I'm good enough, now I'm ready to be saved." God would say to you, "Go back and sit down. I can't save you. They that are whole need not a physician. They that are good need not to be saved. They that are self-righteous don't need me. If you are well you don't need a spiritual doctor." Men come to Christ as they are.

He who had known no sin became sin for me. Listen. He who had never sinned, became sin. In one awesome experience in six hours on the cross this world shall never comprehend, Jesus became sin. That's why the Bible says, "As Moses lifted the serpent in the wilderness, even so must the Son of man [Christ] be lifted up." Why a snake? Why a serpent? Why not a lily, why not a symbol of something beautiful? Because Christ became sin. That was my sin on the cross. Jesus became sin so that God could pour out his wrath and his judgment on sin on him. The Bible says in Isaiah, "His visage [his facial countenance] was marred beyond that of any man, that we esteemed him not." The literal rendition is this: "He was almost beastly." Almost inhuman to look upon him. Because he was sin. God made Christ "sin" for six hours on the cross. Put his judgment on my sins, on the body of his own Son, on the cross. That's what we mean when we sing "Jesus paid it all; all to him I owe. Sin had left a crimson stain, he washed it white as snow." Not good enough, but bad enough, not attaining it, but because I cannot attain, not giving me advice, he took my part.

A sailor came to the captain of a ship and said, "Sir, my little dog has fallen overboard. Will you stop that I might rescue him?" He said, "Son, this ship does not stop for a dog." The young man said, "Sir, if it were a man would you stop?" He said, "We would." Immediately the boy himself jumped overboard. He rescued the dog and waited for the captain to rescue them both. He took the part of the animal. He identified himself with him. Jesus Christ didn't stand on the sidelines and give advice. He became sin. He came into the ditch of sin. He took my part and lifted me out, by the love of God.

A Chinaman was saved years ago, and came to America to give his testimony. He said it like this. "I had walked through the road of life, and had fallen into a great ditch of sin. Muhammadanism came along and said, 'You're not really in that ditch, you just think you're there.' Buddhism came along, and Buddha said to me, 'Here are seven steps by which you can get out of that ditch. If you will climb and struggle you will come out.' " He said, "I strove, but I could not. Confucius came by and said, 'Here are ten steps of self-attainment by which you can get out of the ditch. If you can come half of the way, I'll come the other half, and take you out.' But struggle as I would, I still was in my sin, hopeless and helpless. Then one day the Nazarene came by. And Jesus saw my condition. He saw the problem. Without a word of advice, he stripped himself of those regal robes of royalty. He stepped to the earth through the womb of the virgin, he that had never sinned, became sin, he got down in the ditch, he got into the muck, got in the mud, got into sin, and he lifted me up. Thank God, what I could not do for myself, Christ did for me. 'From sinking sand he lifted me. With tender hand he lifted me. For in loving-kindness Jesus came my soul and mercy to reclaim. And from the depth of sin and shame by grace he lifted me.' I didn't lift myself. He didn't tell me how to get out. He didn't advise, he didn't philosophize, he didn't theorize, he got under me and he lifted me out." Such is the nature of the love of God. The love of God is unattainable. You cannot struggle and improve yourself and get up to it. You can only open your heart to Jesus Christ and let him in. And let him do in and for and through you what you could never do for yourself.

Then the love of God, ladies and gentlemen, is inexhaustible. I'm glad that there is still room. Think of it like this. For God so loved the world, put your name in there. For God so loved Bill Jones, Susie

Marshall, or Peter Johnson, that he gave his only begotten Son, that whosoever, put your name in there, if
Peter Johnson or Bill Jones would believe on him,
would not perish, that Bill Jones, or Peter Johnson
would have everlasting life. Because, you see, I believe with all my heart that just as it takes no more of
the blood of Christ to cleanse the hardest sinner, and
it takes no less of the blood of Christ to forgive the
smallest child, that if I were the only sinner in all the
world, Jesus Christ would have still have come from
heaven's glory and died on the cross for me. Because
God so loved the world, the person, the individual,
me, that he came for me, he would have come had I
been the only one. But I thank God that though he
would have come for only one, that the last drop of
blood that flowed from Emmanual's veins is still as
effective and effectual and powerful to cleanse the
vilest sins of all who will come.

And when the last soul has been saved before Jesus
Christ comes in judgment, there will still be provision
and mercy and grace and plenty for all who would
come and respond in faith to the love of God.

Now the last word is this. The love of God is inevitable. I mean by that that it just had to be. The
Bible says that God is love. This does not mean that
God is an abstraction or a philosophical persuasion,
such as envy, or sincerity, or failure, or success, or
pity. But it means that the totality of the personality
of God is of such vastness, of such loveness and love-
liness and lovingness that he just could not stand by
and watch man, distanced from God by sin, lost and
separated in spiritual death, and his great heart not be
moved to become the divine initiator, the great origi-
nator, and bring about my salvation.

For the wages of sin is death, and dead men like dead wood that cannot grow flowers, cannot produce goodness and life that seeks up after God. So, God in Christ came seeking man. And the gospel is simply this: That he loved me so much that his son died on the cross, and if I open my heart and let him in and experience his love and give him my life and love in return, I can be pardoned; I can be a child of God, justified before my heavenly Father, and rightly related to God by faith in Jesus Christ.

Some years ago a great preacher in Boston had an experience that he told all over the world which I think is so descriptive of all I have been trying to tell to you in these brief remarks. Dr. A. J. Gordon said that one day as he came out of his church, he saw a little boy standing in the alley with a cage. And in the cage were some little field birds, wrens, and sparrows and little things that he had captured. And he said, "Son, what are you going to do with them?" "Well," he said, just like a little old freckled nose boy, "look here mister," as he pulled one of their wings. "I like to make them scream. I'm going to torture them and have some fun, then I'm going to feed them to the cats." "Well," Dr. Gordon said, "Son, I'd like to have those birds." He said, "You mister, you don't want these birds. They ain't no good for nothing." "Well," he said, "Son, I was a boy like you once, I know them, I know their names, I recognize their voices and the color of their eggs. I'd love to have them." He said, "Mister, you'd have to pay for them." "Well," Dr. Gordon thought, "a young enterprising businessman." He said, "All right, how much?" He said, "You wouldn't pay it." He said, "I'll pay anything you ask." "Really?" And so as though he thought he had asked for the world, he said, "Five whole dollars!" "Well," Dr. Gordon said, "that isn't too bad." He reached into his pocket and paid the price and took the birds. He said the boy went his way and as he stood there he realized that there he was, a dignified pastor of a big church, standing in the alley with a cage of birds. Now, the WMU ladies might come out and see him and think that he had lost his mind. So he thought he had better do something with them. So he said he went over behind his car and raised up his trunk, sort of like he was leaning on it so that no one would see him, and he opened the door so that the birds could fly out, but they just froze. Afraid of what they did not know, they just huddled and would not move. Dr. Gordon said he nudged one of them and he was afraid, but he finally flew. And then he circled and sang as though to say, "I'm free, I'm free." Then the others followed one after the other.

Dr. Gordon said that that reminded him that in college he had heard a Chinese legend that said one day Jesus was walking across heaven. He came up to Satan and Satan had a cage full of sinners. And he said, "Lucifer, what have you got there?" Satan said, "I've got the world, I've got all of mankind." He said, "What are you going to do with them?" "I'm going to promise them everything, I'm going to promise them the moon, but then I'm going to break their hearts and damn their souls, and send them into hell without God." Jesus said, "Satan, I would like to have them." He said, "Jesus, you don't want them. They'll steal your money, they'll desecrate your day, they'll blaspheme your name, they'll break your promises, they'll dance in your blood, they'll break your heart. You don't want them." He said, "I want them. I know the numbers of the hairs on their heads, I know their names, I know their next thought before they think it." He said, "You will have to pay." Jesus said, "I'll give you gold, the gold of all the universe." "No, no, no, no not enough!" "I'll give wealth, pearls, rubies, of all the mountains and of all the oceans." "Not enough." "I'll give you diamonds, the diamonds of every world, and every hemisphere. I'll give it all to you." "That's not enough, not enough." "All right, Lucifer, name your price. What do you want?" Legend says that Jesus stood there and Satan said, "You wouldn't pay that!" He said, "Name it." Lucifer said, "All right," as his lips curled in a scowl, "I want gold all right, I want the gold of your heart. I want diamonds all right, I want diamonds of your tears. I want rubies all right, I want the rubies of your blood. I want you, Jesus, on a cross. But you won't pay it." Then, without a word, Jesus began to lay aside his royal robes, came to the earth, lived a perfect life, and went to the old rugged cross and bled and died and poured out his life on Calvary for every man and woman and boy and girl, for whosoever will.

For God so loved the world. By his own blood and by his own cross he opened the door, he set the captive out of captivity, he set bondage to freedom, he builded a bridge back to heaven by the way of the old rugged cross, by which men can still be saved, can still walk toward that glorious place called heaven.

But you know, the preacher tells people they are free, God opens the door, the word of God goes out, the invitation comes in and men sit there and freeze. But sometimes the Holy Spirit of God will tug extra hard and somebody will come and walk through that gate. And they will come back and say, "Why, it's true. It's better than I thought. It's wonderful." Then the next one comes, and the next one, and the next one. They all join singing, "Redeemed, how I love to proclaim it, redeemed, by the blood of the Lamb." Because God so loved the world.

What of you tonight? Mercy's door is still ajar. Have you experienced the love of God? Will you come with the myriad hosts who have come through the centuries? Will you come and open your heart with the many hundreds who are here who have already experienced His love and say, "Oh, God, let that blood fall on me. Let that love come into my heart. I open my heart to you, Lord Jesus, come in and be thou my Savior."

9

For This Cause Came I

When Jesus Christ was in the garden, they came to him as to a thief. They came with spears and swords, and he said, "No man can take my life. Why come you out against me as though to take a thief? Don't you know that if I desired to do so, I could call down legions of angels from heaven? They would come and deliver me from this hour. No, but for this cause came I unto this hour." And he went willingly to the cross. And he went willingly to die. He did not go under constraint. It was no side issue with him. It was no accident. It was not as Albert Phitzer, contemporary liberal theologian says, "an accident that got away from God, and before he knew it, the whole plan had gone astray and was out of his control." And he reasons thusly that God is not a good God, because he could have saved him but he didn't. Or else he is not an omnipotent God because he wanted to save him but he couldn't. But it was no accident that he came to die. He went willingly to the cross.

And there were also two other malefactors led with him to be put to the death. And when they were come to the place that is called Calvary, there they crucified him. And the malefactors, one on the right hand and one on the left. Then said, Jesus, "Father, forgive them for they know not what they do."

And they derided him. And they said, "He saved

others, let him save himself if he be the chosen of God." The soldiers also mocked him, coming to him and offering him vinegar. Saying, "If thou be the Christ, save thyself and us."

Jesus answered not a word. They wrote a superscription over him in letters of Hebrew and Latin and Greek, "This is the King of the Jews." And one of the malefactors that was hanged railed on him and said, "If thou be Christ save thyself and us." But the other answering rebuked him saying, "Dost thou not fear God? Seeing thou hast the same condemnation? And we indeed justly. For we receive the due reward of our deeds. But this man has done nothing amiss." And he turned to Jesus and said, "Lord, remember me when thou cometh into thy kingdom."

And Jesus answered and said unto him, "Verily, verily I say to thee, today thou shalt be with me in paradise." And the sun was darkened, and the veil of the temple was rent in the midst. And Jesus cried with a loud voice, "Eloi, Eloi, la-ma sa-bach-tha-ni," "My God, why hast thou forsaken me?" And he said, "Into thy hands I commend my spirit." Having said thus, he gave up the ghost.

What is this scene on Calvary? Is it as some have said, an accident? A mere historic tragedy? Like the drinking of the hemlock? Or the assassination of a great king? Or the death of Julius Caesar? What is this on the cross? Is this merely another event from which calendars are dated either one way or the other? Is this as some have said, a mere figment of the imagination of man? The product of Greek mythology? That black day that in reality never really ever happened. Some have said that it was just another dramatic presentation, like King Lear. Or Strange Interlude;

or the Agamendum of Eskulus. And it really has no power to save, no relevance today. For after all a dead carpenter hanging naked on a piece of wood couldn't answer my problems, forgive my sins, and change my life today. I am contemporary and I must be relevant. All of my neurosis and psychosis, and all of my inhibitions and hangups really have no disillusion in a piece of wood, and the man that hung upon it two thousand years ago.

But that's not what the Bible says. Oh, to be sure he was the great creator of Christian ethics. He was the master psychologist. For he who had created the human heart knew more about it than any psychologist that ever lived. He was the great social reformer. But even his own contemporaries continually misunderstood the purpose for which he came.

Yonder after the resurrection, the Bible tells us in the book of Acts that they came to him and said, "Lord Jesus, wilt thou at this time restore the kingdom to Israel? Now, will you re-establish the Christian community? Now, will you bring social reform? Now, will the kingdom of God come upon the earth?" And he said, "It is not for you to know the signs and the times of the seasons. But ye shall be my witnesses. The poor you will always have. Get about the business of evangelism. For what does it profit a man if he gain the whole world and lose his own soul?"

No man ever marveled at his wisdom and not come to drink of the mystery of those awesome words that coursed from his lips. No man was ever touched by the passing garment of the Galilean ever again to be the same. For though some were against him and rejected him, driving them to their own ultimate insanity, some to the deserts, some to the mountaintops, where they wrung their hands again and again, washing their hands of the blood of Jesus. Though some followed him into hell for a heavenly cause, though some loved, though some hated him, none were ever neutral who ever once met the Galilean.

But though with all of these things he charmed the women, he excited the men, he thrilled the children, he raptured the teen-ager, and none were ever neutral that ever saw this man live. Though the bowels of the earth rumbled, and the centurion who stood by the cross as a part of the Quaternion guard that had nailed him to the gibbet had said, "I never saw a man like this before." Yet it was for none of these things that he came! How Baptists had better remember that. It is on the keen cutting edge of evangelism, not the hot butter of social reform that we have made an indention into our society, and shall rise or fall in the future.

Jesus Christ summing it all up said this is no by-product for me. "This is the reason why I came into the world to die." To live, yes. Saved by his life, yes. Why? Because his life was perfect. Had it been imperfect, his blood would have been impotent to save. But the perfection of his life validated the power of his death, and the vicarious power of his blood to cleanse and to save.

Napoleon walked again and again, when upon the threshold of conquering the known world, slapping those riding gloves in his hands as he paced to and fro in front of a great map of the world. For in the middle of it was the British Empire encircled with a giant red dot. "There," said Napoleon, "there, if it were not for that red dot, the world would be mine."

Jesus Christ had bled and died upon the cross. It was Monday morning now. Calvary was done. It was finished. Down every little side street in Jerusalem the news came, "The Master is risen." "No," said some, "they have thrown his body away. It is a conspiracy of the Jews, and the Roman officials." But the disciples knew. For in their heart was something they had never known. In their breasts beat a fire they had never known before. And their coursing blood pumping like a thousand racing sand chariots across the floors of heaven within them said, "He is not here. He is risen. He is risen!"

Satan was defeated. Again he, too, walked to and fro reviewing his defeat. What had gone wrong? Now he knew the fatal mistake he had made. Goading again and again, Christ to the cross, prodding those Pharisees to drive him there; forgetting that he who had come from heaven to continue the war against him that had the power of death, sin, hell, and the grave, forgetting that it was not going to be by his life, but by his death. "He would bruise the serpent's head."

Satan had made a mistake. Satan was wrong. And he was impotent and drained of his ability, his strength, and his capacity to enslave, doom, and damn.

Jesus had cried, "It is finished." And Satan thought he had won. But he was wrong. He had lost. That was not the cry of futility. That was not the cry of a coward. Not the cry of fear. That was the cry of a hero. That was a champion's call. That was the victor's cry. I've been into hell; I've been into death. I've wrestled and grappled with the powers of death, hell, sin, and the grave. I am the resurrection! I am the light and life. And he that believeth in me, though he were dead, by my death he shall live. Because in some mysterious, transcendent way we shall never comprehend, for these things desire the angels to look into, he who had never sinned became sin! And he died.

"God," says Isaiah, "took his judgment and smashed it upon him on the cross. And his anger and his judgment upon sin and the sinner were placed on him." The Hebrew word is *smashed* on him, the iniquity of us all. That was me on the cross; that was you on the cross. That was God circumventing every difficulty, by-stepping every excuse, going to the heart of what he knew to be the problem and changing human personality by a complete rejuvenation of human character, by faith in that blood that removes sin and makes a man a child of God related by new birth, to the heavenly Father. "For this cause came I into the world."

For this cause, for this hour. He would not miss it. The Son of Man has come to seek that which was lost, lost, lost! What an awful word it was. Never before had it meant what it meant then. When man sinned, the creation fell. There was sin everywhere and its ugly stain. It was all about God's beautiful universe. For he never made anything imperfect. In the beginning, God created the heaven, perfection (Gen. 1:2). And the earth was—no—the earth became (Hebrew) without form and void. Satan had touched it. The cry had gone up around the triune, trinitarian council tables of God. They knew that day would come before the earth's foundations were laid. They knew that one day the cry would come. And in advance God so loved the world that he planned, the preordained, that his beloved Son would come and die upon the cross. And now it was done. Because man, man the creature, man the creation, man the being made in the image of God, seeking to live, had to die. Seeking for life, had found death. Trying to climb, had fallen; looking for the best, had found the worst. But God said, "I will redeem man." And now it was done!

Ah, but before Calvary, there was Saturday, and the silence of death. Before Easter, there was the silence of the dead tomb of Saturday; before that was the awful ignominious suffering, the pain God laid on him for the iniquity of us all. Calvary. Before that there was Gethsemane. He had gone into Gethsemane to pray, that was where he said it. "For this cause came I." This is where he prayed. He had never sinned. He had known no sin. And yet he was going to become sin. He was going to have to become me; he was going to have to become you. So that God could lay his chastisement and his stripes on him for me. On him for you! On him for us!

He knew that. He prayed because of one last dying struggle. The divinity and the humanity of Jesus vied for survival. He was tempted in all points like as are we. He did not want to die, yet he came willingly to die. And he knew he must die.

The Bible says of that night, great drops as it were of blood burst from his brow as he prayed, "Oh, my God, Oh, my Father, if it be possible if there be any other way, let this cup pass from me." Of what cup was he speaking? The pain of every childbirth, the disease of every twisted body, the suffering of every sinful heart, the death of every dying body, the disappointment of every brokenhearted mother, the tear of every father, the disillusionment of every sin was now placed into one cup. Placed to the lips of a thrice-holy God. And he drank and drank and drank it to its bitter dregs. And blood and sweat mingled and trickled down the throat of a thrice-holy God, as one last battle takes place in his breast to bring the flesh under submission in the garden of Gethsemane. It seemed that every imp of hell was there, and every demon from the penitentiary of the damned brought all their power to get him to escape this hour. And they came against him with swords and spears. But he said, "I have come for this hour."

"You'll not take me by constraint. I'll pay the price, for the redemption of that little girl and that little boy, that teen-ager and that young husband. For this cause came I into the world."

And he said, "Don't you know if I wanted to, I could call twelve legions of angels? They would fight for me. They would deliver me from this hour. They would give me escape from this misery. They would free me from this moment." And that number to which he referred, somewhere between fifty thousand and a hundred and fifty thousand, is but a minute part of the angelic host that would have come to fight if but a breath, if but a word, a prayer, if but a thought had gone out from him to them. Had he even looked into the face of his Father, all of the angels of heaven would have come bursting from the precipice of glory to save him from that hour. To take him on transcendent wings of angelic power back to the royal diadem from whence he had come. But he was not done with his task.

And why shouldn't they come? They loved him. They had ministered to him. Thousands upon thousands stand before him, says the psalmist. And as Daniel the prophet says, "Ten thousand times ten thousand stand before him." They would have come. They loved him. They were the angelic choir that joined that first Christmas night, "Peace on earth, good news, good will toward men." They were there, they walked with him, they protected him as a little boy across the streams as he forded the rivers and climbed the mountains as but a Jewish lad playing about the carpenter shop.

They were there as he broke the bread and fed the five thousand. They walked with him. The angels that came and destroyed Sennacherib's army would have destroyed the world had he wanted. Why shouldn't they come? Those same angels that were to stand by the tomb for that glorious proclamation, "He is not here, He is risen." The angels that stand before him as he sanctifies the throne with his blood as the mercy seat is sprinkled again and again. They would have come. Those angels that will come with him when he will come with flaming fire taking vengeance and judgment on them that know not God. They would have come and saved him from that hour.

And why shouldn't they? For everything else in nature responded to the cross. The bowels of the earth began to rumble. The tombs split. The dead arose. The rocks cracked. The veil divided. The sky turned black. The Father turned his head and everything in creation responded to the cross, but the angels. They were the last chance. They vied and strained. "Let us go. Let us save him." But he said, "Oh, no. I didn't come to pass out a few biscuits and penicillin. I didn't come to teach you some little rose-water ethics about how to live. No man's going to separate me from that for which I came." Jesus Christ was simply saying I can do more by dying for the world, than I can by feeding it; by teaching it; and healing it. For the problems that plague us and damn us and defeat us, are the problems of the human heart.

Only the blood can by faith fall upon me, touch my

stony heart, save me, do the job for me. Only the blood! He had to shed his blood!

And he went to the cross willingly.

At 9:00 on Friday morning they crucified him; but not before a trial. Not once, but thrice was he tried. Yonder in trials that were erroneous in over fifty points of the Roman law. Without notice, without witness, without publicity, without benefit of counsel, under the veil of night; before Pilate, before Herod, back again before Pilate. "I find no fault in this man. I find no fault in Jesus Christ." Again and again they cried, "Release Barabbas anyway; let Jesus be crucified."

Simon of Cyrene watched. Tears coursed his cheeks, as the cat-o'-nine-tails bit into his back and emaciated it. And he stumbled up Golgotha's hill with that seamless robe that they had laid on him in mockery, pricking their own fingers first with a crown of thorns, saying, "You're a king. Well, a king needs a crown," cramming it upon his head. He stumbles and falls. And that giant bronze figure walks to the side and says, "I'll carry his cross." A three hundred pound cross was put to his back, now broken, now torn. They come to the top of the mountain and he says, "Turn loose of my hand. I lay my life down freely. No man takes my life. I came for this cause."

Those hands that were raised as he said, "Let the little children come unto me," now were nailed. Again, steel bites flesh, as reverberating down the corridors of time the echoing sound: "The world is crucifying the Prince of glory." The hand that was raised when he said, "Peace, be still," and "Peace I give you," now was stretched as tightly as a drum head, now the other hand is laid upon the beam of the cross and a spike again bites the flesh and rising to fall again in judgmental execution the deathblow of the executionary mallot.

The feet that had carried him to preach the gospel of freedom and good news to the poor, of him that was now poor, that for our sakes we might be made rich, now were crossed. A fifteen-inch spike is placed through both of them. Again they pound the nail into his cross. He writhes in agony. And he looks down and cries, "Father, forgive them; they don't know what they do."

And thank God, two thousand years later he is still in the business of saying, "Father, forgive them. Forgive them."

They arched his back with a cruel instrument of torture placed in the middle of the cross, that ripped the lungs from their moorings, that made it possible to exhale but impossible to inhale, for one would strangle on his own blood.

He bowed his head and said, "It is finished." His hands are now limp, his eyes now glazed in death, look with open lid to the face of his Father. Blood ran down his side, past his precious leg, and trickled from his pierced feet. It fell on the dust of the earth. And said "It is finished."

And the dust said to the grass, "It is finished. It is finished." The grass said to the flower, "It is finished. It is finished." The flowers whispered to the trees, "It is finished." Trees raising their boughs on high join, "It is finished. It is finished!" And angels laying aside their royal instruments of music, step to the edge of heaven and join in the refrain, "It is finished." And every bird says, "It is finished." The saints hear, 'It is finished." The bowels of the earth rumble, "It is finished." And the dead say, "It is finished." And the living say, "It is finished. It is finished. It is finished."

But he arose! He ever liveth to make intercession. He is good, he is a philosopher, the great psychologist, the master sociologist, the ultimate healer, Jesus Christ himself. He gave the focal point, that crux and zenith, the core and apex of all of organized religion that every Methodist and Baptist and Lutheran and Assembly of God and Presbyterian and Episcopal layman and rector and preacher and teacher among us is called and bound under God to acclaim and proclaim until he dies; it is for this cause he came! To bleed on the gibbet, to die on the cross, to suffer on Calvary. To put himself out a ransom for many on the old rugged cross.

Some laughed. The covetous sat down and began to gamble beneath the cross. The Pharisees wagged their tongues and walked up and down, and danced and pranced again and again their satanic tune. They laughed and mocked and jeered. "Now, where's your savior? Now, what will your dead carpenter do?"

Some went back to the fishing nets. Some wept. Some said, "I told you so." And some came and said, "Let's wait a minute, maybe there will be some more show, maybe there's a little more show to go on here. Let's come and see whether Elias will come and save him. Maybe we will see another miracle, another trick, and we'll all have a good time."

But I think those that broke his heart the most, were those that just stood there in stolid indifference as if to say, "So, what? So, what?" Is this not what prompted the prophet of old to say, "Is it nothing to you, all ye that pass by?" And the Corinthian writer again to add, "You before whose very eyes Christ has evidently been set forth."

What is it to you? And I add, can you ever be the

same, having touched him? Can you ever again be neutral having seen him? Can you ever again stand and do nothing having heard, please God by the Spirit's power, the cross vivified and visualized before your very eyes? What will you do with Jesus? Walk away?

In the beginning was the Word. Jesus. And the Word, Jesus, was with God. And the Word was God, Jesus. All things were made by him, Jesus. And without him, Jesus, was not anything made that was made. He was in the world, and the world was made by him, but the world knew him not. He came to his own, and his own received him not. But as many as received him, to them gave he power! Power! Power to become the sons of God. Because the enmity that stands between God and man is slain on the cross.

If you will receive him, you may have him. You cannot be neutral. That life-giving power will come in, save you, forgive and bless and change and translate and transport your life. It is not enough to have a steeple with a cross on top of a church. It is not enough to have a pretty sign, "We preach Christ." It is not enough to have a trinket on a dashboard. Not enough to have a good-luck charm on a bracelet. Not enough to sing in a choir "The Old Rugged Cross." It must be experienced. His power will be in your life if in faith, you will step from that barbarous crowd. Yes, you are there; we are all there. Step in faith to the foot of the cross, and say, "Oh, Lord Jesus, let it fall on me, let your blood touch my heart. Oh, Lamb of God, I come. I come."

10

The Plan of Salvation

In 1 Corinthians 15:1-4 the apostle has given us God's interpretation of the gospel. The plan of salvation is here stated. If I were to ask you what it means to be a Christian, or what it means to be saved, what would you say?

Stop hundreds of people on the street of any city on any given day and ask them what it means to be a Christian, and you might be surprised at the different answers. If this auditorium were filled with unsaved people from all over the world, who had never heard the gospel, how many of you could sit down and in everyday simple language explain to them the plan of salvation? What does it mean to be saved? What does it mean to be a Christian? What is this business of religion all about?

Most of the time I feel that we preachers assume that our people know what we are talking about. And that when we use big words like glorification and justification, and when we use such theological expressions as lost and saved and conversion and incarnation and resurrection that we just assume that everyone knows what we are talking about. When, in reality, they may not know at all.

I want us to pretend that you have never heard the gospel. I want to explain to you as simply as I know how, what it means to be a Christian, and what the plan of salvation is all about. Now I know that most of us have gone to church all of our lives, and have developed a little habit of sort of tuning in and out what the preacher is saying. And what we have in the conclusion is merely a hodgepodge of disassociated facts, most of which don't really add up to anything.

What is religion all about? What is the plan of salvation? If you can do so I want your mind to ramble back through the corridors of time back to a place where there was no earth, no starts, back to the very, very beginning. Can you imagine a time when there was absolute black, empty vastness, absolutely nothing, no cars, no television sets, no people, no moon, no sun. The Bible says it was like this in the beginning. But there was in the beginning God. Now, you say preacher, "I'm already hung up. I don't understand what you are talking about. How could it be that God always was?"

The word "everlasting" means without ending. We have everlasting life. In Christ we have no ending, but we did have a beginning. There was a time when we were not. But the Bible tells us that with God there was never a time that he was not. He is eternal. That is, he has no beginning and no ending. You say, "I don't understand that." "I don't see how that can be." Neither do I; neither does anybody else. And you never will, so just forget it. Suffice it to say that we have to give God credit for knowing some things that we don't know. If we could answer all the questions, if we could explain everything there is to explain about God, then we could be God or at least be his equal, and we could not worship him. How God always was is one of those things that I do not understand, I cannot explain, but that I merely accept.

In the beginning God. Now, the Bible gives us some

insight into God's personality. The Bible tells us that God likes to be worshiped. If I have the desire that I want to be praised, and admired and worshiped, that may be sinful, but with God it is not. I don't understand how it is, but I do know that God wants his creatures to worship him. I do think that the reason is that we might have the joy that comes from worshiping him. In other words, it is for our benefit, and not for his.

And then also the Bible tells us that God is hungry for the fellowship of people. God wants people to love and honor and worship and serve him; and he wants people with whom he can fellowship. And so God created this world. Now, whether there is life in other planets, I do not know. But I do know it could not be any higher type than the life on our planet. Because we are made in the image of God. And you just cannot be any higher than to be made in the image of God. If there is life on other worlds, it could not be superior to ours. This world is God's supreme creation. And man God's supreme creature. God made this world. It was to this world that Jesus came. The Bible says that when man fell all of creation fell with him. And so, if there is life on other planets, it is fallen too. But it was to this earth that Christ came. It was to man that Christ came. Now, to have fellowship with man, God must make man like he himself is. And so the Bible tells us that God made man in his own image.

This does not mean that God has arms and legs and eyes although the Bible speaks, perhaps symbolically, of the hands of God and the eyes of God, saying that the hand of God is always extended toward us in mercy and forgiveness, the eyes of God are always upon us. But basically it means that God has some particular

capacities that make him *personality*. And he created
and endowed us with the same capacity.

One, God has knowledge; he knows things.

Two, he has emotions; that is, he feels things.

Three, he has a will; he does things.

Now, the will of God, the things that God does, are
based upon a rational and an intelligent combination
of what he knows and what he feels. Animals do things,
but they do not have a free will, they are not able to
reason and make intelligent decisions based upon what
they know and feel. They have conditioned responses;
they do things automatically. It is not the result of
intelligent reasoning and human rationality.

And so God having knowledge, emotion, and will, is
above the animals and is above the creatures; and so,
he made man above the animals. The light and counte-
nance of God are upon the face of the human being. He
made man in his image with knowledge, emotion, and
will.

When God placed man upon the earth, he said,
"I want you to subdue the earth and replenish the earth
and have dominion over it." God gave man a beautiful
paradise in which to live. They tell us that at the
North Pole today they have found icebergs that contain
tropical plants indicating that once the world was an
equatorial paradise. Many theorize that it was perhaps
an equal 72 degrees all over the world. For God never
made anything that he did not make perfect, and in
the beginning God created the heavens and the earth.

Now, Genesis 1:2 says that the earth was without
form and void. But the literal rendition of the Hebrew
word is this: But the earth *became* without form and
void. In other words, the earth fell. The Bible says
that all of creation fell. God did not make the earth

imperfect. It became void and empty and imperfect. What happened? Satan touched the earth as he touched man and they became imperfect as everything that he touches falls and becomes imperfect.

If God wanted to, he could have made man a robot; he could have wound him up and told him what he had to do. But because God wanted man to live on the highest plane, on the highest level, he made man a free moral agent. That is, he did not say "You have to have fellowship with me. You have to worship me." He gave man a free will and said, "You can choose to serve me." Because he knew that if man served him willingly because he chose to and not because he had to, man would be happier than he would if he had not the privilege to choose to serve God. But God knew that he ran the built-in risk that man would also choose wrongly and harm himself.

If I give my children roller skates I am enhancing their opportunity to live happily. For if they learn to use those roller skates properly, then they will be happier than they would be if they didn't have roller skates. But I am running the built-in risk that they will use the skates wrongly, and fall down and hurt themselves.

And so God took the risk, knowing the end from the beginning, knowing the Lamb of God waiting in the wings was slain from the foundation of the world. And because he loved man, he would come to take the initiative and come to man and provide for his salvation if, and when, he fell. God made man. He created him from the dust of the earth. He breathed into him the breath of life.

The Bible tells us that when God created man, a free moral agent with knowledge, emotion, and will, the devil came to man and said, "God is withholding from your spiritual good. God is your enemy. Follow him and die. Serve me and you'll live. I'm the way to have real life." And so man listened to Satan. Immediately, he sinned and fell.

The result of man's sin was death. Once there was life in man. The life and light of God. Created for God, he lived in perfect fellowship with God. But now, because of sin, God left the heart of man. And man, distanced from God by sin, was now empty and dark and dead and impotent and lifeless.

But the Bible tells us that God loves man so much that he did not want man to remain in a state of spiritual death. He wanted him to live. So once again God, the great initiator, the great instigator, moves into action to recreate man, to provide for man's salvation and to restore man and justify man again into his original position of being rightly related to God who created him and loved him and who would one day give himself for him.

Now, man being dead, needing to live, could come to life in one of two ways. Man could struggle and strain and bring himself to life, if it were possible. But a dead piece of wood cannot grow a beautiful flower. And man's heart distanced from God by sin, dead in trespasses, iniquity, and sin, is now dead, sterile, lifeless, and impotent. And death cannot produce life. And so man devises a hundred ways by which to gain life. And by his own good works he strives and struggles, but the Bible says that he can do nothing to produce life. The wages of sin is death. Death can only produce death. If a dead piece of wood could be brought to life, since it cannot create life and generate life within itself, the only possible way that it can be brought to life is that some greater power would superimpose itself upon it and bring it to life. And so that is what God decided to do.

He said, "I will bring man to life." But God had a problem. Man was a sinner. God being a sovereign God could not ignore man's sins. He could not overlook man's sins. "Just forget about it. I'll save you anyway. I'll forgive you anyway." God is a sovereign God. That means that he not only has the privilege of making laws, but has the obligation of enforcing those laws. God had created his own law, the result of sin was death, and now God must operate within those laws, and could not ignore man's sins. He could not just forget about them. He must deal with the matter of sin.

But man, because God loves man, could not create life within himself, and all that he could do would be to remain in a state of death. God said, "I will provide for man." "I will give man life." But that meant taking care of the problem that had caused death, the problem of sin. So, God must pay for man's sins. He must remove man's sins. He must in some manner deal with the problem of sin in the heart of man.

And so now God was faced with another problem. If God was going to forgive and remove the sin of man, God being a perfect God, did not accept anything for the provision of man's sin except absolute perfection. But now that sin was in the universe, there was nothing left that was perfect. Even the earth had fallen. There were no thorns on the roses before sin. There were no weeds in the field before sin. But now imperfection was everywhere. There was nothing left in the world that was perfect. No perfection in all of the universe. Nothing to be man's substitute, nothing that a perfect God would accept. Except one thing! God himself was perfect. But no! A thousand times no! That's not reasonable! That doesn't seem right. That doesn't seem feasible. That God himself would die for man's sins. But thank God that is exactly what God decided to do. He said, "I will provide for man's sins. I will pay for man's sins. I will be the great substitute."

But that left God with another problem. The Bible says that God is a spirit. And they that worship him must worship him in spirit and in truth. A spirit could not pay for my sins. A spirit could not die on a cross. A spirit could not bleed and suffer the shame and horror of a terrible bloody cross. And so God had to have a body. God the great spirit, God the Father, had to become a man. And so God looked around, and his eyes fell upon Mary. There in her womb he decided to provide himself a body. And the Bible says that God breathed upon her and the power of the Almighty overshadowed her and she was with child of the Holy Ghost. And that holy thing that was formed within her womb, says the Word of God, was the very God of very Gods, the divine Creator become a man. God incarnate in human flesh. And when Jesus Christ was born, he was no ambassador from God, he was no spokesman from God, he did not represent God. He was God, incarnate in human flesh. Jesus Christ was God come down to earth. The word made flesh, Logos, Emmanuel, God with us, God in a body. When Jesus Christ walked on the water, when he fed the five thousand, when he was nailed on the cross, when he went into the tomb, that was God living, breathing, existing, dying in a body. And so Jesus Christ went to the cross. God's perfect substitute for the sins of the world bled and died. That's why we sing with joy and thanksgiving, "Jesus paid it all, all to him I owe. Sin had left a crimson stain, He washed it white as snow." Thank God my sins are paid. The blood atones for my transgressions. God in Christ has been my substitute. That's wonderful news.

You say, "Praise the Lord, preacher, let's stand and go home. That is indeed wonderful news." But ladies and gentlemen, that's not quite all. There's one other thing! You must accept in faith what has been done for you. God has paid for your sins, and now he offers to you that finished payment. But you must accept it. Suppose some of these children here tonight were to go to the store and buy some candy? I could come along and say, "I love those children, I'll pay their bill." "They charged that candy, but put that on my account." Now you youngsters could come to Brother John and say, "No, I don't want your old payment, you just keep that money." Or they could say, "Yes, I love you, Brother John, I'll accept your payment." Will you accept it or reject it? It is yours, but it's no good to you if you don't take it.

If I offered you a hundred dollar check, it would be worth a hundred dollars. But it would not be worth a hundred dollars to you personally until you endorse it, until you write your name there, until you accept it by faith. Then it is not only good, but it is good to you personally!

Jesus Christ has written the check of eternal life to you. He offers it to you. He says, "I have paid for your sins. It is finished; it is done; I have paid it all on the cross." But you must accept it, you've got to write your name on that blank. You must receive Christ and what he has done for you on the cross. You must receive in faith the gift of God. Will you do it?

He says, "I stand at the door and knock. If any man hear my voice and open the door, I will come in and sup with him and he with me." I urge you with all of my heart to open your heart and receive the gift of God. We all are sinners by choice. God moved to provide for man's sin. In Christ on the cross, Jesus paid it all. He arose from the grave, he's alive, he's every where, he is here tonight, he's standing at your heart's door. He wants to come in. He will if you will let him.

11

How to Be Saved

In Romans 10:8, the apostle Paul is discussing the law, the Scripture, the Word of God. And he says regarding that Word, "What saith it?" And here is the answer, what the Word of God has to say. "The word is nigh thee, even in thy mouth, and in thy heart: that is, the word of faith, which we preach; that if thou shalt confess with thy mouth the Lord Jesus, and believe in thine heart that God hath raised him from the dead, thou shalt be saved. For with the heart man believeth unto righteousness; and with the mouth confession is made unto salvation.

"For the scripture saith, Whosoever believeth on him shall not be ashamed.

"For there is no difference between the Jew and the Greek: for the same Lord over all is rich unto all that call upon him.

"For whosoever shall call upon the name of the Lord shall be saved" (vv. 11-13).

I said in an earlier message that just before the coming of Jesus Christ there would become a tremendous amount of confusion in the world as to the way of salvation. You ask a number of people in the streets of this city how is one saved, and you'll get many different answers. Some will say, "Be baptized." Some will say, "Count your beads and do good works." Some will say, "Join the church"; others, "Take your catechism, make your confession, be baptized, take of the Lord's Supper, merely think positively, or it's all a state of mind." And many will deny that there is a God, a heaven, a hell, or the reality of salvation at all.

But I believe as intelligent men and women, you believe in these things and you believe in being saved. Then, what is the problem? The problem is that there are many that have never been saved. I have asked the question from east to west, and I have never found anybody who has said, "I've made up my mind, I believe there's a hell and a heaven, and I'm going to go to hell. I don't want to be saved. I don't ever intend to be saved." Most people have the good sense to desire salvation. But if there is a great amount of understanding as to the motivation for salvation, then there is a great controversy as to the method. And so tonight I want to crystalize in your minds the ABC's of how one is saved. I'm going to give you five steps.

Now, we say that salvation only entails one thing, believing on Jesus Christ. This is true. But there are some steps that lead up to the time that a person is ready to make a genuine committal of his heart and life to Jesus Christ.

1. Before you can be saved you have to realize that you are lost. To be saved means to be saved from something and it means to be saved to something. It is an awful thing for a man to be lost. It means to lose his potential; it means to come short; it means to end up in the final analysis not having completed what God had in mind for your life. I don't know, but I think when we get to heaven somehow God may have a beautiful silver screen in which he shows us the wonderful plan he had for our lives, what he wanted for us, and what he had planned for our lives. What

we could have had. And as sin means missing the mark, then we shall see how far short we fell of the glory of God. Now, that verse that says all have sinned and come short of the glory of God doesn't mean that we could be as glorious as God is. I believe it means we have come short of the glory God has for us. God is not our enemy. Any minister of religion has to struggle with that lie. It is the same temptation, it is the same malicious lie with which Satan originally came to man, that God is withholding from man's good. "Follow me and live," he says; "follow Christ and die." He wants you to be miserable. He wants you to have a lousy time in life. He wants life to be terrible and dull. "But if you'll follow me," says Satan, "we'll really live." But man, in trying to follow him, found he was really following death. And the result of sin is coming short of the glorious wonderful life that God has for man. To be lost means to lose. To be lost means to miss. To be lost means to come up short. To be lost means to be discarded, rejected; a loser, a dropout. You will never know what life is really all about until you find it in Jesus Christ.

When I was fourteen years of age, I was the youngest professional dance band leader in America. I had nine grown men working in my employ. By the time I had graduated from high school, I'd made two and three thousand dollars in one night. I've done shows with King Cole, Doris Day, Peggy Lee, Ray Anthony, Woody Herman, and I had everything a teen-age boy's heart could desire. But I had to acknowledge that after all there was something missing on the inside. I was made in the image of God. I was made for God and I had left God out. I was never really quite satisfied.

Don Demeter, the great baseball player for many

years the center fielder with the Tigers, Phillies, and Dodgers, said, "When I was twenty-six, I had hit three home runs in one game, I had been in the All-Star games three times, I had the legal limit in most of the Oklahoma City banks, but there was an empty spot inside of me, a vacuum. I tried to put everything inside of there, and then I realized that that vacuum was God-shaped. And nothing would fit it but God." Man is made in the image of God. He is made by God and for God.

Emmanuel Kant says that the final proof of God is why does man never find his ultimate rest until he finds it in God. He may be the president of a great organization, he may be a multimillionaire or a president, but ladies and gentlemen and teen-agers, until you find your rest in God, until you get Christ in your life, you will remain lost, you will be losing all God has for you. You will come out second rate. You will come up short. You will miss the boat. And what God does is merely to abide by your decision in attempting to serve the devil and leave out God in this life. But if you follow Christ in this life, and are saved, then you follow him into eternity in the next life!

Now if you are satisfied with nothing, if you are satisfied with being gypped and cheated at the devil's bargain table, if you are satisfied to live in your sins, to waste your life, to rebel against God, to die and go to hell, God has made you a free moral agent, you are free to choose that if you wish. He could have dropped a nickle in your ear, wound you up every morning, and made you a mechanical robot, but he didn't. He gave you the free right of choice. And you are lost by choice. We live without God because we want to. And that is your privilege. You can live that way. But it is to waste your life. It is to be cheated. It is to be short-changed. To be lost is to lose. And you're going to have to become dissatisfied with coming up on the short end of life. You will never be saved until you realize you are lost.

2. Having realized you are lost, the next step is simply this: You must desire to be saved. I've seen thousands of people start up that long road to heaven because somebody came to them and said, "I love you, I want to see you saved." Last week in the football stadium of Del City we had about 210 people saved. The week before that it was my privilege to be in the revival in a football stadium, in an Encounter Crusade in Corsicana, Texas. Several hundred people were saved in that meeting. All over the country I've seen thousands start for Christ because someone went to them and said, "I love you, I care about you, I want to see you saved, I'll go with you." But in the final analysis, it must be you who willingly responds. You must want to be saved, you must desire to be saved. Nobody can push you into it.

Thank God for Sunday School teachers who agonize and weep and pray over lost souls, and plead with God for the conversion of their class members. It's wonderful to see a teacher come down the aisle bearing her precious jewels, bringing them to the feet of the cross. Saying, "Here Lord, here is one I have won and brought to you, as Andrew brought his brother, as all wise men have done through the centuries." But in the final analysis, you must come to Christ because you want to. You are a free moral agent, it is your will. You can come down the aisle to get the preacher off your neck, get the Sunday School teachers to leave you alone, make a lip profession of faith. But the Bible says,

"Out of the abundance of the heart the mouth speaketh." And what the mouth says when you say "I believe on Jesus Christ; I commit myself to him" must be the result of what you really and genuinely mean in your heart.

In the book of John at the close of chapter 2 we find a very interesting story. The Bible says many believed on his name when they saw the miracles that he did. But he did not commit himself unto them. That looks like a great revival was sweeping the country. That would make headlines in any denominational newspaper. Wonderful! Great! Many believed on Jesus. But the Bible says, "He committed not himself to them." The word "commit" the writer uses is the exact word he had just used when he said "believed." In other words, many believed in him, but he did not believe in them. Why? It's right in the text. They believed only when they saw the miracles. They only believed for a superfluous reason. It was not genuine. They wanted to go along with the crowd. They wanted to see part of the show.

As some stood by the cross they thought that Jesus cried for the prophet. And they said, "Wait a minute, let us come and see if Elijah will save him." But he was crying for his Father! They misunderstood. For they said, "Let's see what will happen. Let's hang around for the show. Who knows, maybe a prophet will rise from the dead. Maybe something exciting will happen."

They were just there for the show. They were just there for the miracles. They were just there for spurious reasons. They had missed the fact that saving faith must come from the heart. One must want Christ. Now, you may want to please your parents. You may have come down an aisle because a teacher asked you to, but that doesn't mean that you're saved. You can't be saved against your will. I thank God for those who say, "I'll go with you," and motivate us. And we do so many things that motivate people wrongly in life; thank God for good motivation. But first you must realize that you're lost, and you must desire to be saved! You must want it. If you want to die and go to hell and waste your life, and sit on the back row and say no to the preacher, you can. But I think that the wisest, the most wonderful, the most rational, intelligent thing that you can do is want to be saved!

3. You must repent of your sin. Now, I didn't say sins. I said sin. Understand, we all have a rebellious nature about us. The nature of sin, the principle of sin, is operative in the life of every individual. As a result of that we commit sins, individual and specific sins. Now, it does no more good for a Catholic to come down and say I did this and I did that and think he is saved, to confess all of his sins, than it does for a Baptist to do that. No, sir. That doesn't get you salvation. You don't need to enumerate your sins. Some people come down and say, "Well, Lord, forgive me. I got drunk last Saturday night. I been jay walking. I been cussing out the old man, spitting in the sink, reading dirty books, I've been doing everything." And they just rattle off all their sins. Now, that doesn't get the job done. You don't need to deal as a lost person with the fact that you commit specific sins.

You need to acknowledge before God that you are lost and that the totality of your entire personality is one of sin. We are basically sinners. It is our tendency to go away from God. "Lord, my whole life is against thee. God, do not forgive me for what I do, but forgive me for what I am, a willing sinner, in rebellion and against you." You must repent of your sin. The direction of your life has been away from God. It means to stop, turn, do an about-face, and go to God. Repentance gives up yourself to God. And what yourself does will take care of what you are when Christ comes in and give you a new nature. Let me ask you a question. Have you genuinely repented of your sin? You might have filled out a card and nodded your head to some questions. But have you made a life-changing decision where you repented, where your life was transformed?

After I was saved, I went back to my hometown. I had the same hair, the same legs, the same feet, the same eyes, but the members of my band thought I was crazy. "What happened to Bisagno?" they said. "That's not the same guy we used to know. Has he gone crazy?" I didn't go to the same places. I didn't act the same way. I was a new person. Christ had come in. I had repented. I was different. I was changed. I was redirected. I was transformed. Has that happened in your life? Have you been born again? Have you repented? Have you quit going away from God, with the totality of your nature now going to God? That's New Testament repentance.

And so, one must realize that he is lost. He must desire to be saved. He must repent of his sin.

4. And you must ask Jesus Christ, in faith, to come into your heart. Ask God for the gift of salvation.

How would you offer salvation? God did it through the most obvious and wonderful and equal vehicle in all of the world. The ability to believe through faith. By grace are ye saved, that's the basis of our salvation. Faith is the vehicle of our salvation. That's the way we receive salvation. "You mean by merely believing that a carpenter died and rose again two thousand years ago, I can be saved?" I mean exactly that. If you are willing to say, "I do believe that Christ was the Son of God, that he lived, that he died for my sins, that he was my Savior, and that I want to trust my soul, my sins, my life, my future, all to Christ, in faith I believe he will save me, he will come into my heart! I believe that he will forgive my sins. I believe that he will take me to heaven." Because Jesus Christ, the greatest gentleman that ever lived, who cannot lie because he was the truth, incarnate in human flesh, said, "I will come into your heart if you will ask me to and I believe him," you will be saved. Will you believe that?

The Bible says, "Whosoever shall call upon the name of the Lord shall be saved." Now you don't know me from Adam. I could be a phoney. I could lie to you like crazy. I could make up all kinds of promises. Men are men. But ladies and gentlemen, Jesus Christ never lies. Circumstances change. Emotions change. Feelings change. But thank God, though the heavens and earth pass away, the Word of God will never change. And it says, "Whosoever shall call upon the name of the Lord shall be saved." And so if tonight you understand, that never having received Christ and had a new birth experience, you are lost. You realize that it isn't particularly smart to want to waste your life and die and go to hell. You want to be saved. If you are willing to repent of your sins, your life principle that goes in opposition to the will of God, turn in faith to God, then if you are willing to ask Christ to come into your life, the Bible says, you will be saved.

There are only two kinds of persons. Those going to

heaven and those not. Those with Christ and those
without him. The saved and the lost. All the boys and
girls, the teen-agers, the mothers and dads fall into
either of those two categories. The saved or the lost.
I'm going to ask you tonight if you want to be saved,
to receive Jesus Christ as your Savior. Do you realize
you're lost and have never been saved? Do you desire
to be saved? Are you willing to give yourself to God?
Are you willing to ask Christ to come into your heart?
Listen, again. "Behold I stand at the door and knock,
if any man hear my voice and open the door, I will
come in. But as many as received Him, to them gave
He them the power to become the Sons of God. For
whosoever shall call upon the name of the Lord shall
be saved." Children, teen-agers, moms and dads, it's
not smart to waste your life. It is the most normal, reasonable, rational, wonderful, intelligent, sensible decision in the world to ask Christ to come into your heart.
Listen. Will you do it right now? Confess Christ before
men. Did not our Lord himself say, "Whosoever therefore shall confess me before men, him will I confess
also before my Father which is in heaven. But whosoever shall deny me before men, him will I also deny
before my Father which is in heaven."

12

The Kingdom of God

My text is just one verse of Scripture and in a moment we shall read it together. Revelation 11:15. "And the seventh angel sounded; and there were great voices in heaven, saying, the kingdoms of this world are become the kingdoms of our Lord, and of his Christ; and he shall reign for ever and ever."

Exiled for the Word of God to the Isle of Patmos, John was given a special revelation. And God showed him what things were going to be like at the end of the world; as it shall be then, when it is actually going on. And so the word "are" would better be translated for our use today, "have."

And the seventh angel sounded; and there were great voices in heaven, saying, "The kingdoms of this world have become the kingdoms of our Lord, and of his Christ; and he shall reign for ever and ever."

The idea of a literal kingdom of God on earth as such with a literal king reigning over that kingdom was probably not in the heart and mind of God originally, but perhaps grew in response to a need in the hearts of God's people, the Israelites. Though they were special they are and were still very ordinary people, with plain ordinary people's failings and inconsistencies. The Jews noted that their neighbors, whether friend or foe, had certain things that they did not have. They had idols, so the Jews wanted idols.

They had certain methods of government, so they wanted the same thing. They had armies, and so the Jews wanted armies. They had a king and so God's people wanted a king. Not at all unlike us today. So, God decided that he would honor the request of his people and the Jews were given a king.

First, there was Saul who reigned for forty years. Saul greatly desired to build a house for the glory of God, but he failed as did David, his successor, who also ruled for forty years. And then there was Solomon who was successful in building the house of God, as he ruled, completing the 120 years triune dynasty of these three men. Now, under Solomon, the Bible tells us that the kingdoms divided. In the north there were ten tribes, the tribes of the Israelites, and in the south, the southern kingdoms composed of Benjamin and Judah composing the Judaic tribes. And yonder they had 19 different kings to follow as did the tribes of the north. The Davidic dynasty continued through nine generations. But although they had tremendous results in the advent of their successors, one after another, still all of them together, did not do much better than did those southern kings. And in the final analysis and the final report of what God did for man when God was willing to do what man wanted done for himself, was a complete and abject failure. For not one of them made the success and was the embodiment of everything that the Jews had desired and hoped that a king would be.

Then God did a wonderful thing. He sent his only begotten Son, the Son of God, Jesus Christ, to become all that they wanted. And the King of kings, the Lord of lords, very God of very God—God in Christ became King. And God gave men a real king, sure enough king, who was to rule and reign forever. But the strangest thing in all of the Word of God happened, for when God sent them the perfect king, they rejected him. For they in reality, like most of us, did not know what they wanted at all. But Jesus still was the King. He was a very different king. And he came to reveal to us what the kingdom of God is really like.

And Jesus taught us some important truths revealing the nature of the kingdom of God that God has in mind for the world.

Three words for your memory that will help us to understand the nature of the kingdom of God which Jesus, the King of kings, came to establish and rule over in the hearts of men.

First of all the kingdom of God is internal. Now, this was hard for them. They didn't understand that. The Bible says that God is a spirit. And they that worship him must worship him in spirit and in truth. Man made in the image of God is a spiritual being. And he never seems to learn that life doesn't consist of the abundance of things that he possesses. Man seeks after the physical, the material, the literal when man, a spirit, being made in the image of a spirit God must ultimately be satisfied with a spiritual fulfilment of his spiritual desires. The kingdom of God is among you and it is within you. But man has not changed through the years and he still wants his Gods and his realities to be physical and tangible and touchable.

But Jesus said the kingdom of God is within you. The kingdom of God is not what you had expected. It is an internal kingdom. It is the kingdom of the human heart. And it is by the willing enthronement of the King of kings as Lord of the heart that the kingdom of God is established daily in every believer who comes to Jesus Christ.

The Roman writer said it like this. "The kingdom of God is not meat and drink. The kingdom of God is righteousness and peace and joy in the Holy Ghost." Now, let's look at that. The kingdom of God is not what we touch and eat and feel and see. It is first righteousness, then peace, then joy in the Holy Ghost. Man's philosophy says if I can *have* I will *be* happy. Jesus said, "If you *are* you will be happy." If we *are* certain things. Not if we possess certain things. Now, what are these certain things? First, there is righteousness. The kingdom of God is righteousness. First of all to enter in faith to a literal relationship to a literal God that gives literal fulfilment, one must be something. That is, one must *be righteous*. Then he says when we *are* righteous, then we will *have* something.

The world says seek something, have something, then you will be something, then you will be happy. Jesus says be something then you will have something. Then will you have what you want. So, we must first of all be righteous.

Now, he says when we are righteous, and we have peace, he says then you will have something more than that. Then you will have a good time. Joy in the Holy Ghost means fun, pressed down, running over, good measure. The Christian life literally can be a gas. But first of all there must be righteousness. You must be something, then you will feel something, then you will feel everything. Righteousness, then peace, then more than peace, joy in the Holy Spirit of God. The kingdom of God starts in the human heart. And so the kingdom of God is internal.

Then, secondly, the kingdom of God is supernal.

Now, I don't know that you will find that in the dictionary. You'll find it in my dictionary, but you might not find it in yours. The word means supernatural. Above the natural, beyond the natural, different from the nature of the ordinary.

Now he says that I'm coming to establish my kingdom differently than you would do it. It is above the ordinary. It is beyond man.

And all through his beautiful philosophy of life revealed in the Sermon on the Mount, Jesus changes things. He says that it is different than you think. My ways are not your ways, my thoughts are not your thoughts. I do not do things as you do them. And so he tells us that the kingdom of God is supernal, it is above us, it is different.

When Jesus came, they wanted to make him a physical king. And so they placed him on the back of a donkey. They gave him a scepter and a robe, and they planted a crown upon his brow, and rode him triumphantly into Jerusalem, expecting the immediate overthrow of the kingdoms of this world.

But Jesus was saying all the time that the kingdom of God is not in pomp and ceremony; it is not in palm leaves and parades; it is not in processions; the kingdom of God is different from all that. But they never did understand it. They wanted to make him a literal king from the very first. He raised the dead, he fed the poor, and it looked like a winner for sure. One woman came and said, "Lord, let one of my sons sit on your right hand. Let's have him be the first vice-president." Another said, "Lord, let my other son be second vice-president." I can imagine that impetuous Peter must have said, "Lord, I'll organize a Navy." Another said, "I'll start the army," another said, "I'll keep the book." Judas came in and said, "I'll count the money, I'll be the treasurer. We won't have to ever work again. We've got a king. He'll go around. He'll raise the dead, everybody will join up. We won't have to work any more. He'll turn rocks into bread. And we will feed the poor, we'll never have to suffer. He'll take care of our needs. Let's crown him king."

But Jesus said, "You don't understand!" And over and over again he tried to teach them that the supernal nature of the kingdom of God was unique and different from anything that the world had ever tried to comprehend before.

Napoleon the Frenchman and Genghis Khan the Oriental had come. They had run roughshod over the armies of the world, and the Christians oppressed and suppressed were hoping for that kind of a king. "Crown him king." They cried, "Let us rule the world!"

They didn't understand, and so they put him on the cross and he died. And even Peter one of his most faithful followers said, "The king is dead. It is a mistake. I go fishing!" That word "go" means to continually, to perpetually go on fishing. He didn't say, "I'm going to take off this afternoon and fish." But rather, "I am giving myself, I am committing myself back over to a life of fishing. The king is dead. The kingdom is in shambles. It was all a mistake. I am going back to a life of fishing."

Even after the resurrection of Jesus they still didn't understand. In the first chapter of Acts the disciples came and said, "Now, Lord, wilt thou restore the kingdom unto Israel? Is it time for us to rise up?"

"But," Jesus said, "it is not for you to know the signs, not for you to know the times and the seasons. You be my witnesses. You want to get in on the kingdom of

God? Tell people about me! And get me and saving faith in me down in the hearts of your fellowmen. Then the kingdom of God will come on earth." The kingdom of God is supernal, because it changes the heart of man.

Throughout history man had said happiness is to be strong. Jesus said, "Blessed are you when you are meek." History had said blessed are the mighty. Jesus said. "Blessed are the poor in spirit." History said blessed are the strong, blessed are the ones that run over each other. Jesus said. "Blessed are the humble in heart, and blessed are the poor in spirit." The world had said blessed are you when you go to war. Jesus said, "Blessed are you when you are a peacemaker. Because then you are like I am, and you enter into the joy of your Lord." The world had said blessed are you when you are rich. He said, "Blessed are you when you don't have anything, because then you will have to know what it means to trust me." They had said blessed are you when everybody says you're great and all praise your name and you are famous. Jesus said, "Blessed are you when nobody likes your name and they swear and revile you. But they do it for my sake!" Then you will know what it means to be a real Christian. Then you will know what it means to draw on the real sustenance of the Lily of the Valley, and to take succor at his breast.

The kingdom of God was so far removed from what they had understood. I wonder if many of us today still understand what he meant?

One last word. The kingdom of God, thank God, is eternal. Of his kingdom there shall be no end. "And the kingdoms of this world." Now, that does not mean only the literal, the physical kingdoms of this world.

It doesn't only mean the Chinese and the British and the Americans shall all bow and crown him King of kings and Lord of lords, but the kingdom of materialism as well, and the kingdom of entertainment as well, the kingdom of society, the kingdom of finance, the kingdom of politics, the kingdom of education, the kingdom of science, will all one day join together and bow the knee and the kingdoms of this world will be the kingdoms of our Lord!

Let's look at it again. It was in Revelation 11:6. "And I saw," he says, "the seventh angel sounded and there were great voices in heaven, saying, the kingdoms of this world have become the kingdoms of our Lord, and of his Christ; and he shall reign until the United Nations gets into trouble, until the united counsel of churches fixes all of our problems, he shall reign until the devil grasps us from his hand?" No! A thousand times no! He shall reign forever and forever, and of his kingdom there shall be no end. The kingdom of God is an eternal one, the kingdom of the heart, the kingdom of righteousness, established in the repentant heart by faith in the living God. It shall never change; it is irrevocable, unchangeable, immutable. Oh, listen to me. When you touch this kingdom, you touch greatness. When the Spirit of God brings into your heart by faith, the presence of the King of kings, you touch eternity. You shall never perish. We shall reign with him. We shall be with him. For we shall be like him. We shall be like him forever and ever.

It is indeed an eternal kingdom. He is going to come and we are going to reign with him a thousand years. And the Bible says that heaven and earth will pass away, then he is going to rejuvenate the whole thing and start all over again. And after we have reigned with him a thousand years, he is going to throw in eternity for good measure!

Is it any wonder that he said, "Eye hath not seen, nor ear heard, neither have entered into the heart of man, the things which God hath prepared for them that love him."

Friend, if you are not on his side, you are on the wrong side. You don't know what you are losing. You don't know what you are missing out on. Of his kingdom there shall be no end.

Alexander the Great, after he had conquered the known world, walked into the ocean and wept, because as a young man of only twenty-nine years of age, there were no worlds left to conquer.

Ah, but when Jesus comes, he will reign forever. He will go on conquering. There was an end to the kingdom of Alexander the Great, but there will be no end to the kingdom of the King of kings, and the Lord of lords.

And we will reign with him if we know him, and have him in our heart. That's what we offer in Jesus Christ.

Christian, take fresh courage; saint of God, take new heart. You who are not Christians, you who do not know the Lord, you'd better get on the winning side, you'd better get into the kingdom of God. You can enlist by faith.